I.W.A.I

and the

Waterways of Ireland

Written and compiled by

Brian Cassells

First published by Cottage Publications,
an imprint of Laurel Cottage Ltd.
Ballyhay, Donaghadee, N. Ireland 2014.
Copyrights Reserved.
© Text Brian Cassells 2014.
Design & origination in N. Ireland.
Printed & bound in China
ISBN 978 1 900935 97 5

"When an old person dies, a Library is burned."

Old African Proverb

For Lilja and Emilia:
hopefully one day you too will enjoy Papa's passion.

This publication seeks to celebrate 60 years of The Inland Waterways Association of Ireland. From its primitive beginnings at the first meeting in 1954, which was attended by over 200 volunteers, a group of like minded people had the foresight to come together with a shared aim of promoting traffic on the rivers and canals, opposing any obstructions and to set up a campaign for the conservation and in particular the preservation of a working navigation.

It is with great pride that I can say today that sixty years later the IWAI has grown to a membership in excess of 3,500. We continue the great work of our predecessors and as an Association we have achieved many great feats and overcome many challenges. No challenge greater than that of our founder members who fought the building of low bridges to ensure that we can still enjoy free access on the inland waterways from Beleek to Limerick and further afield. This is down to the commitment of each and every member of the Association who are no different to our founder members and their shared love of our waterways

This book is a marvellous insight into the Association and a formal record of our sixty year history. Credit must be given to former President of the Association, Brian Cassells for the enormous amount of time and effort he has put into compiling this great book

I am secure in the knowledge that IWAI will continue in its work due to the commitment and enthusiasm of members and the good working relationships with all the agencies involved on the waterways

Enjoy the book

Carmel Meegan
President IWAI

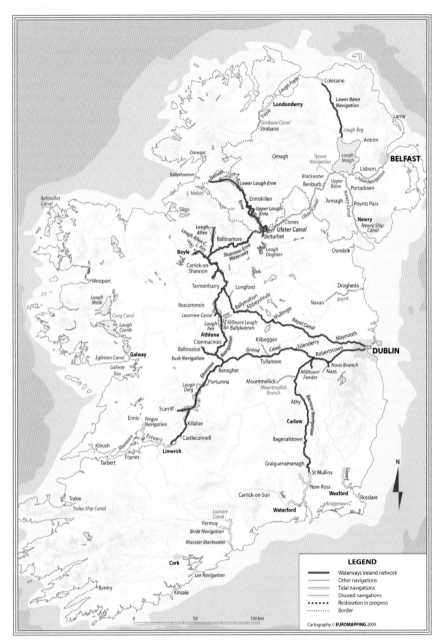

The Waterways of Ireland

Courtesy of Euromapping

Contents

Swans at Enniskillen

Preface and Acknowledgements

This book is the idea of Carmel Meegan, the current President of the Inland Waterways Association of Ireland (IWAI); it was she who approached me first and always had the faith that I could deliver the project, a work that has taken the best part of two years. My appeal to the branches for individual histories took an enormous amount of effort; dare I even suggest it was like getting blood from a stone; target dates were set, and passed but we got there in the end, I hope you enjoy seeing your effort in print. Carmel Meegan, President and Derry Smith our Vice President were amazing, we spoke at least weekly and slowly squeezed the text from contributors, it certainly wasn't easy!

I must state at the outset, grateful thanks are due to the following: Conor Meegan and Martin Donnelly, who have been in touch since virtually the inception of the book, they enquired, encouraged and were always supportive; Damien Delaney and Padraic O Brolchain who were especially helpful; and to my proof-reading sister, Florence who never complained, even though this isn't her subject, willingly read and re-read with her red teachers' marker poised!

I really feel it is so important to get history recorded before it is forgotten, I remember talking to Denis McCartney who kept the Scarva Branch going virtually single handed. Denis epitomised

Enniskillen Castle

for me, the true spirit of IWAI; someone who passionately believed in the restoration of his waterway, the Newry Canal, thankfully that spirit still remains today. Padraic O Brolchain sent me what I understand is an old African saying; "When an old person dies, a library is burned." never a truer statement was made! One regret in life that I have is that I didn't ask my parents and those older folk around me, more questions; sadly when we are young we don't appreciate the vast knowledge the older generation have. Never be too busy to spend quality time with your parents/grandparents or knowledgeable older people, ask questions while you still can, remember time waits for no man and time passes so quickly; if we are not careful, it can be too late!

Ruth Delany and Dr Ian Bath have been founts of knowledge for me for many years. At the outset when researching for this book, I went down to Dun Laoghaire, Ian collected me from the train and I spent the day with both discussing my ideas. As ever, Ruth sent me home with lots to read and research, promising to read over and comment on the final draft. Towards finishing the text I returned to check what had been written, again the welcome and hospitality were amazing, thank you Ruth and Ian for your help, support and encouragement, any success the book may achieve is yours to share.

My study, where I keep my books and write is at the back of my garage, I don't really watch television, I read and I write so most nights Maree sat alone while I worked; it is a big sacrifice I know; thanks Maree for being so understanding, perhaps the peace you enjoyed was worth it, only you dare say!

Finally I want to dedicate this book to all the folk I have met over many, many years, on the rivers, lakes and canals, at meetings and conferences; friends I will never forget. What an amazing experience, what wonderful people whom I am privileged to know! Thank you for welcoming me into this amazing Association!

The following is a list of names, contributors; thanks to each and every one; some have been friends for many years, others I have never met but to all, sincere thanks, I just hope you feel this book has a part in our history and that you all have contributed to that story.

Thanks To Contributors For Text And Photographs

Alison Alderton, Tom Bailey, Dr Ian Bath, Kay Baxter, Colin Beattie, Colin Becker, Siobhan Bigley, Myles Brady, Damian Broomhead, thanks to Colman Byrne; IWAI webmaster, for permission to use pictures taken by the late Roy Redpath, Kathleen Cross, Damien Delaney, Ruth Delany, Brian Denham, John Dimond, John Dolan, Martin Donnelly, Charles Dunn, Bill Eagleston, Michael Farrell, Andy Fitzsimons, Geraldine Foley; Paul Garland, Reggie Goodbody, Peter Griffen, Sam Herraghty, Jim Henning, Michael J Hynes, F. Kennedy for 'Syd and the Saints' picture, Alan Kelly, Jean Kennedy, Arthur Keppel, David Killeen, Siobhan Kinahan, Charles Kinney, Ger Loughlin, Natalie Magowan, Tom Maher, Catherine Malone, Michael Martin, David Edwards May of Euro-mapping, Thomas McIlvenna , Carmel Meegan, Conor Meegan, Robert Navan, Padraic O Brolchain, Gerry O'Hara, Beth O'Loughlin, Lord Raymond O'Neill, Donal O'Siochain, Brian Redmond, Tim Rolt for L T C Rolt photographs, Stephen Rooke, Tile Films Ltd., Michael Savage, Paul J Scannell, Peter Scott of Lagan Canal Trust, Michael Slevin, Derry Smyth, Noel Spaine, John Suitor, Helen Timon, Alistair Uprichard, A. J. Vosse, Dick Warner, Derek Whelan, Declan Walsh.

Executive January 2014-06-06
Left to right; back row; Brian Cassells, Paul Garland, Noel Griffen, Greg Whelan, Martin Donnelly, Derry Smyth, Mike Kingston, Tommy McLoughlin
Left to right; front row; Kay Baxter, Carmel Meegan, Jean Kennedy, Maria Stuart.

Thanks are also due to Tim Johnston of Cottage Publications and Jane Crosbie Lyle for editing. Finally to Carmel and the Executive who have given total support throughout the project. Apologies to anyone who is disappointed not to see their contribution in print; that was an editorial decision not taken by me. I'm sure I have left someone out, please accept my apology; I tried!

*Waterways ireland, the navigation
authority, Headquarters at Enniskillen*

Introduction

To write a history of the Inland Waterways Association of Ireland could be relatively easy, by simply writing up the Chronology of events that is on the home page of our web site, but no, I think our organization deserves more of a story, after all this Association is about real people, those with a determination to succeed, those with a passion to save a slice of history, those who had a vision that the dying commercialism of our waterways could be reborn as a new industry, that of tourism.

In the 1950s in both Northern and Southern jurisdictions, dealing with government departments was very different from today. In the North the Association largely dealt with Rivers Agency, while in the Republic the picture was less obvious; the Grand Canal system and Barrow navigation merged into the transport authority, CIE which had already administered the Royal Canal since 1944 while the Shannon navigation was managed by the Office of Public Works (OPW). In 1986 the Grand Canal, Barrow and Royal Canal were transferred from CIE to OPW and in 1996 were transferred to the new Arts, Heritage & the Gaeltacht (Irish speaking areas) as the Waterway Service. In 1997 it became the Department of Arts, Heritage, Gaeltacht & the Islands which established Duchas, the Heritage Service and waterways were included as Duchas Waterways.

In 2000, following the Good Friday agreement, the new cross border body, Waterways Ireland (WI) was established to administer all the navigable waterways on the island of Ireland under the North South Ministerial Council though they didn't actually assume responsibility until 2002. Waterways Ireland was responsible to the Ministry of Culture Arts and Leisure in Northern Ireland and the Department of Community Rural and Gaeltacht Affairs in the Republic. In the North, WI were responsible for the Erne system, the Lower Bann and tasked with taking forward the study into the re-opening of the Ulster Canal while the remaining once navigable waterways were classified as abandoned and managed by Rivers Agency. In the Republic, WI administered the Shannon system, the Grand, the Royal and the Barrow; other navigations such as the Corrib, the Slaney etc were managed independently.

Sadly all too few who joined that fledgling group are with us today, IWAI is now sixty years old and still going strong and that is quite an achievement in itself. There have been highs and lows, successes and failures, controversial decisions, membership fluctuations, changes in the administration of our waterways and our own public profile has dramatically changed. Yet despite all, the Association forges onward, the early days were undoubtedly hugely successful, then we had an era of consolidation, even at times expansion, we've established new branches in areas where dereliction has frustrated local enthusiasts, leaders have come and gone each leaving their stamp on an Association; that has and is still evolving.

I realise history can be a 'dry' topic hence I have endeavoured to include recollections of those who have been associated with our waterways over a lifetime, people with memories, folk with a story that if not recorded will be lost forever.

Over the years I was privileged to know some legendary people who have given so much to our Association, dare I single out one who to me was the greatest of all, someone I was privileged to call my friend, Ruth Delany and from whom I have learnt so much.

Ruth tells us our story begins with the great English waterway writer and pioneer L T C Rolt. The IWA had been formed in England in 1949, the same year that Rolt published his book, *Green and Silver*; this seemed to awaken a passion which personified itself, firstly in letters in the national press and then with a group of impassioned individuals determined to oppose the authorities changing forever uninterrupted passage on the River Shannon and the impending closure of the network of waterways. Thankfully they succeeded, and some say the battle has been won. I'm not so sure, the threat of water abstraction, of invasive species and of the need to carefully monitor planning along with watching legislation may well mean our role is changing but the membership

The Rolt family on board their narrow boat "Cressy" dining alfresco

need to be as vigilant today as ever; complacency could be our downfall.

The waterways of Ireland have long been a resource for everyone to enjoy, we still enjoy relative freedom from over-regulation and at present boating is affordable to all. In this cash strapped modern era we must guard against those in authority making this the prerogative of the privileged few, the battle is still not won, the foot soldiers need to be alert with a watchful eye.

Tom Rolt on the tiller of "Cressy"

Lock at the Cutts, Lower Bann

The Waterways of Ireland

I've had the privilege to sail most of the navigable waterways of Ireland, from Coleraine to Lough Neagh, with its associated rivers, from Belleek to Limerick and onwards to Dingle, most of the Grand and Royal Canals, the Barrow, the Corrib and Slaney. To quote a favourite would offend some, so I will endeavour to give an overview of what I enjoyed.

Starting in the North the Lower Bann is without doubt an experience not to be missed. To be honest I've always made this journey south to north, starting at Toome and finishing at Coleraine marina, if you get the chance do include the estuary section out as far as the bar mouth and Castlerock. I always associate the Coleraine area and estuary with a great friend, sadly now deceased, Victor Hamill. Victor lived on the banks of the river, perhaps his real passion was rowing; oh how proud Victor would have been at the Olympic success of the Chambers brothers. The estuary section is wide with a well-marked channel, teeming with wild life, bordered with sand dunes and relatively sheltered. If you attempt to leave the river through the walled bar mouth take advice, be careful of tide over-flow, a few spare horsepower in the engine can come in useful!

Heading down river from the bridges of Coleraine, the Cutts lock is the introduction to fresh water; between the town and the lock you cross the river, lots to look out for, upwards to Mountsandel where there is a fort which was the site of one of the earliest inhabited areas of Ireland, passing Coleraine's sprawling suburbs on the other bank, you'll be amazed at the abundant wildlife this area has to offer. The unattractive sluice gates dominate the port side view (left for the uninitiated!) look the other way and hug the starboard bank (right). Going through the Cutts Lock, on the starboard side, is the Waterways Ireland office (where the local engineer couldn't be more welcoming and helpful) and past the lovely Georgian House, which is the home of The Honourable, the Irish Society. If you have a moment call with the Chief Executive, he is a fount of knowledge on The Plantation of Ulster, the London companies and their relationship to the city of Derry/Londonderry, indeed the North West of Ulster. The next section of the river is wooded with the banks dotted with desirable waterside dwellings where the gardens tumble to the water's edge often harbouring jetties where the residents' pride and joy awaits release to explore these lovely waters. The navigation splits around Loughlan Island, relax, just follow the well marked channel and all will be well, though the waters of this section of the river can often be lively with speed boats and wake boats; before you complain about the wash, remember the river is for everyone to enjoy so all must respect each other.

The Portna Locks on the Lower Bann can also double as a dry-dock.

Drumaheglis Marina and Caravan Park makes a welcome break, although just to add to the excitement this is the area where seaplanes operate; I've never been really comfortable with that idea, encountering such certainly raises the blood pressure and stress levels! Carnroe lock looms ahead, pick up a copy of the navigation leaflet and phone ahead alerting the lock keepers; regretfully they are never that busy on the Lower Bann. Movanagher lock lies next in a short canal cutting and then comes Portneal Lodge, just before Kilrea. Each time I have made this trip I have over-nighted at Portneal Lodge and this is accommodation and food to recommend; the welcome and hospitality has been commendable all at a very affordable price.

Next comes Portna Locks, look out for the eel traps which remind us of an important though declining asset of the river, the catching of silver eels which are harvested at Movangher, Portna with the largest facility at Toome. The live eels are exported to London, Holland and Germany where they are offered up as delicacies. Another favourite stop of mine is the Wild Duck Inn at Portglenone, here the quality of food has never disappointed, next through the navigation arch and onwards past Newferry, a popular water skiing area and to the gem of the river, Lough Beg. Sailing through this shallow ribbon like lake with the picturesque Church Island is for me the most relaxing enjoyable part of the journey, all too soon the new bridge over the A6 looms gaunt on the skyline then the raggle taggle structure that forms the Toome eel

"Island Warrior" leaving Ram's Island after a litter lift operation.

fishery is on the right hand side, keep left through the navigation arch, you are now in the Toome Canal passing through what once was the Carlisle Railway Bridge and in front lies the last lock on the system.

Beyond the canal lies Lough Neagh, Ulster's inland sea, 26 miles long by 16 miles wide with only two fair sized islands, To navigate the lough requires considerable knowledge and for inclement weather some basic navigation and boat handling skills. For any would be sailor attempting this journey may I recommend a publication from a long standing colleague, Michael Savage; *The River Bann and Lough Neagh Pilot Book*; this gives detailed information on the Lower Bann as well as Lough Neagh. Other than some brief information

on the islands I do not propose to detail Lough Neagh as that has been well covered in my previous publication *By the Shores of Lough Neagh*.

Ram's Island lies off the eastern shoreline and is one of the foremost projects of the Inland Waterways Association of Ireland. The author of the pilot book, Michael Savage is the project co-ordinator of Ram's Island; the island is owned by Lord O'Neill of Shane's Castle and Honorary President of the River Bann and Lough Neagh Branch; it is leased to our branch for a nominal rent which is not collected. Michael operates the branch ferry boat "The Island Warrior" which is berthed at Sandy Bay marina and takes visitors out by pre arrangement and conducts a fascinating and informative tour of the island, showing the topless round tower and the remains of the O'Neill summer house. The only other main island, Coney lies off the southern shores near the mouth of the River Blackwater. Coney Island like Ram's has the remains of a round tower and this time the summer cottage, once belonging to Lord Charlemont, has been refurbished and is inhabited by the warden Peter McClelland. Peter like Michael gives visitors an enthralling insight into the history of this magical place, owned by the National Trust and administered by Craigavon Borough Council.

My boat journey south is impeded by the abandoned Ulster Canal which leaves the River Blackwater just before the village of Moy. Before we leave south Lough Neagh it would be remiss of me not to mention three important abandoned waterways, the Lagan, and the Newry and Coalisland canals. The Lagan leaves Lough Neagh in the south-east corner and connected the lough to Belfast. The recently formed Lagan Canal Trust has been set up to take forward the project of re-opening the canal; the section from Lough Neagh to Moira is relatively easy to re-open as is the section from Sprucefield to Belfast, though here the locks are in a much poorer condition, sadly our enlightened politicians of the 1950s built the M1 motorway over the middle section of the bed of the canal obliterating one of the most iconic aqueducts in Ireland. Progress is certainly being achieved, though in times of austerity imaginative sources to fund the project will be necessary; the adjoining Maze Long Kesh site creates additional possibilities. The towpath is extremely well used by walkers; surely inspired politicians see merit in providing the catalyst which would re-invigorate the Lagan Valley Corridor. Our Lagan Branch, with the fervent support of Lisburn City Council has been pivotal and exemplary in promoting the regeneration of the Lagan Corridor; their founding Chairman Jim Henning displays outstanding leadership.

Arguably the most strategically important waterway in all of these islands is the Newry Canal; the oldest summit canal in all of the United Kingdom and Ireland; it lay in a derelict neglected state until our Association recently formed a branch on the canal. This branch has certainly set the standard for canal regeneration, with work parties organised every third Saturday; the branch Chairman Peter Maxwell has shown outstanding leadership and has earned the reputation of getting things done. Volunteers have removed damaging vegetation from bridges and lock chambers exposing artefacts from a long forgotten era; this waterway was originally opened in 1742 to carry coal from the newly discovered deposits at Coalisland. Like the Lagan, the re-opened towpath is extensively used by cyclists and walkers, thus promoting healthy safe outdoor activity.

The other abandoned Northern waterway in this area is the short Coalisland Canal; this linked the River Blackwater with Coalisland and in many respects was seen as the obvious extension to the Newry. Coalisland as well as producing coal was

Plaque commemorating Jim Canning

notable for its clay products hence the canal provided the necessary highway to export bricks and associated clay products. Here too, the local branch has put this waterway on the National map. The branch was originally started by Jim Canning, a local politician who caught the vision of what a restored waterway could do for the town of which he was so proud; James Walshe endeavours to continue to fulfil the dream of a visionary. Hereto the towpath has been re-instated and is widely used by the local community.

The boat journey west continues by the River Blackwater where the now abandoned Ulster Canal impedes our trip by boat. The Blackwater is one of those amazing undiscovered backwaters, it teems with wildlife, I don't think I have ever seen so many Kingfishers in such a short area. Sadly the M1 Bridge restricts navigation to all but low air draft boats, but the effort is well rewarded.

The old canal leaves the river just before Moy and without local knowledge it is difficult to discern the first lock through the thick vegetation that has now virtually obliterated the entrance. The new proposed Ulster Canal route uses the river as far as Blackwatertown necessitating a short cut to be dug to access the old canal just beyond the village. This project has been high on the agenda of IWAI for the past twenty odd years. It is the "missing link" in the waterway chain which, when opened, will create an enviable, diverse waterway network that will rival any in Western Europe.

It is still possible to trace the waterway to Maydown Bridge which is at the foot of the Benburb gorge, one of the most dramatic areas of any waterway. The Blackwater tumbles to the right of the original seven locks, some now obliterated with others in poor condition. I have always advocated the creation of a boat lift here, a much less expensive option to re-instating the locks but one that would create a tourist hotspot, the "Falkirk Wheel of Ireland". Just imagine boats sailing into a cradle and trundling up and down a vernacular railway. At the top of the gorge is an old mill mothballed but waiting to be re-opened to tell the linen story of Ulster, there is a well preserved steam engine just one of many exhibits to tantalise prospective visitors. The village of Benburb has so much to offer the discerning visitor, the Servite Priory, the historic Church of Ireland with cannon and musket balls from the Battle of Benburb and the Fort not to forget the priory cottages along the main street.

*Ulster Canal
Aqueduct
at Clones*

Leaving Benburb the canal strolls to Caledon where there is the first of the four iconic aqueducts', and then it skirts Lord Caledon's estate, what remains of the Tynan Abbey estate, which was the home of the Stronge family, and the third of these grand landed-gentry seats, Castle Leslie, now a hotel where Sir John spilt the beans about Paul McCartney's wedding! Middletown beckons with a couple of hard to find lock-houses and, at the border, the second of those pretty aqueducts. The filled-in canal section was once the home to a filling station where when fuel was cheaper in the north, the tanks were situated on that side of the border but when the reverse became the norm the tanks were quickly moved across the dividing line! Caledon estate is one of the largest land areas in Northern Ireland having 2400 acres. The

Grand entrance beside the village of Caledon doesn't look as grand today; the pillar was blown up by terrorists early in the 1970s and only the stump remains. Sadly Tynan Abbey has gone too, Sir Norman Stronge and his son James were murdered in 1981 and the house was burned to the ground during the attack. Castle Leslie has been in the Leslie family for generations; the family were cousins of Winston Churchill and traditionally have been prolific writers.

Anita Leslie, daughter of Sir Shane Leslie penned something like seventeen books; she is buried in the small graveyard adjoining the present house. Anita was married to Bill King, who had a distinguished WWII career; they had two of a family, her daughter continues to live in Oranmore,

Sluice house near Quigg Lough

Co. Galway while her son Tarka, a great friend of IWAI and the Ulster Canal, farms an estate in Pentridge, Dorset.

Monaghan beckons but not before the canal and the A3 journey side by side past Monaghan Mushrooms and Tyholland School; here there are some well-preserved examples of those narrow locks complete with winding gear. When I talk about narrow locks it is because one of the major drawbacks of the original canal was the fact the locks were not compatible with the rest of the Irish system, in fact the narrowest was less that twelve feet but taken the fact that the locks will require to be dismantled before they are rebuilt they will be reconstructed to Shannon Erne specifications. At the new road roundabout on the outskirts of Monaghan the engineers had the foresight to not only construct the bridge to modern specifications but also created a ledge for the towpath. I think from here to beyond Monaghan is one of the most exciting stretches of canal and towpath, past the old asylum lock to a rather sad forgotten lock-house behind the hotel and on to Monaghan where the canal skirted the town.

Here the local politicians had the foresight to create a short linear park along the derelict canal, a peaceful haven where the town traffic noise can soften into oblivion. On the other side of the unattractive low bridge lies St Louis convent school, where the former canal stores served as a school gymnasium, then the canal winds its way through what was referred to as the deep cutting. I'm delighted to learn the towpath from the Armagh road roundabout as far as Clones is to be re-opened as a greenway; hopefully it won't be too long before walkers and cyclists enjoy the great outdoors, perhaps this will be the precursor to seeing boats navigate this section...I wish! Beyond Monaghan and near Smithborough lies Quigg Lough which was the feeder lake for this summit waterway; from the perspective of the waterway historian the sluice house is worth the walk, Glear double locks which lie further along on the other side of the main road are pretty impressive with another rather sad looking lock-house though the last time I visited the site, someone had removed some of the cut cap-stone from the lock wall.

Time for coffee, where better than the Canal Stores in Clones, this now boasts a small lace exhibition; indeed there is always a convivial reception here for the weary traveller. I think Clones is an amazing place, Saint Tighearnach is the patron saint

*Ulster Canal
stores at
Clones*

associated with the old abbey and round tower situated just up the street from the Canal Stores. The town with its imposing ancient Celtic cross over-shadowed by the Church has a welcoming feel, the people seem genuinely glad you are there and a real effort has been made by the businesses to spruce up their premises. A visit to the famine graveyard, a short walk from the town centre is worth the effort if only to experience the tranquillity such places can bring. I love the connotations of The Cassandra Hand Centre at Ball Alley Lane, Cassandra was the lady who introduced lace to Clones in the 1840s; it is a gorgeous quaint Gothic styled structure that has been tastefully restored. Leaving Clones on the left hand side is the third of those aqueducts though this particular one is heavily infested with ivy as indeed is the last

one though it necessitates leaving the main road and after some minor roads, negotiating a hedged muddy lane. Eventually the canal reaches Lough Erne, sadly water no longer exits from the dry bed into the Finn River at Derrykerrib, time to resume the water borne journey.

Heading towards the Erne I love the sound of the area known as the Quivvy Waters, the thoughts conjured up make me dream of misty mornings, solitude, at one with nature, time to reflect and dream, indeed to question what life is all about. I don't propose to give a detailed description of the Erne or indeed the Shannon suffice to say if you haven't witnessed the Creighton Tower and the ruins of the old castle at Crom, go, and don't delay, it is quite a special place especially water

The start of the Shannon Erne waterway at Leitrim

borne. The run up to Belturbet and the town itself are well worth a visit, lots of fine hostelries here which can be difficult to leave!

The Shannon Erne waterway beckons, the new century restoration where the locks are operated by a smart card. Gone are the balance beams and rickety clog wheels, as for my opinion on that, the jury is out, I love the heritage but have to admit modern technology makes transition very easy. Ballyconnell, Ballinamore and Keshcarrigan each have their own appeal, I've great memories of an evening spent in Gertie's Bar the year the canal opened, the food was great, the craic was mighty, sadly some of those who were present are no longer with us, isn't it strange you don't really appreciate the magic of the moment at the time; some-

how the memory is that which is so special. The rock cutting, Kilclare Upper, Middle and Lower soon pass and Leitrim Bridge has to be negotiated; this always requires skill as folk do seem to moor up at least two abreast and close to the bridge. I've grave reservations about the developments leaving the town, the dark grey stone gives me a sombre shudder, and rather than call and support the incumbents I feel the urge to make Carrick with all it has to offer.

Now we've reached the water motorway through Ireland, have you ever heard the saying that anyone who is dipped in the River Shannon is said to lose all their bashfulness, no further comment and I'll not name the person who I'm tempted to ask! Decision time; taking right brings us to Acres

"The Fox" moored outside the Irish Army Barracks in Athlone

Lake and hence into Lough Allen. Drumshanbo is worth a wander and for an unforgettable experience visit the Arigina Coalmines where the guides are retired miners. Further along the Shannon another right turn takes you into Lough Key with its attractive forest park and a particularly picturesque island complete with the shell of a castle.

There are no two towns on the Shannon quite like Carrick and Athlone; when I visit Carrick, I have to visit the antiquarian bookshop for the elusive bargain and I can't resist Naughty Bits, a lovely name for a chandlery! Some good restaurants beckon but it's hard not to resist a nosey into the Bush Hotel just to see who may be lurking

in a corner, this hostelry has to be the commercial home of the waterways. Now we really are in a boating paradise, lots to see, lots going on and Moon River slides by taking ordinary people out on the water. Jamestown is next, then Dromod worth a stop to visit the railway and museum; well that's what it's called and next comes Roosky with lifting bridge and lock. Sail on my friend until you see the large chimney at Lanesborough, after the bridge is Lough Ree, an often missed boating opportunity. Lough Ree is long and narrow with lots of islands; lots too of interesting harbours and places to visit; my old friend Reggie Redmond who knew and loved the lake presented me with a bottle of Lecarrow Blackberry wine, I treasure it,

Killaloe

I'll never drink it, the memory of all it conjures up is much too precious!

Athlone beckons; mooring for me is below the Radisson Hotel on the town marina, safe secure moorings and the opportunity to stand and stare at The Fox on the far bank with that huge spotlight sadly silent now without Master Sid, small in stature but mighty on the river and a musician of considerable note. Sid Shine was the skipper of The Fox, a skilled knowledgeable boatman and leader of one of those amazing show bands that played all over Ireland as well as the dance hall run by his late father. I remember Sid at a dinner dance in the Hodson Bay Hotel just outside Athlone dancing not as an Octogenarian would dance, but nimble footed and with perfect rhythm.

I miss being able to call with another old sailor, Sean Fitzsimons, Fitzy sitting at the end of the bar, supposedly the oldest pub in Ireland, Sean's Bar, Sean was ever eager for news, though I always found he had more to tell me than I ever had to tell him. History is my forte, I've walked along the old canal which by-passed the town but who would want to by-pass such an interesting place, the ladies love the shops but I'm always content to wander and dream.

Ruins of the Grand Hotel at Shannon Harbour

Lough Derg like the Erne lakes are my idea of boating; you'll never see them all, there is always something new; the run down to Killaloe from Parker Point with the tree lined shore and the mountains hanging over remind me of "The Graves of the Leinster Men" and Brian Boru's fort, truly magical places to wander back in time and dream of Celtic legends, futile battles fought for what? My friends from that neck of the woods would never forgive me if I didn't mention Terryyglass, Dromineer, Garrykennedy and Mountshannon; take your pick, they are all special, but my personal favourite is Killaloe where the mighty river is the border between Clare and Tipperary.

Now for a surprise statement from a man with a plastic white boat, "I really think I'm a canal man at heart"! The Grand and the Royal not to mention the Barrow are truly amazing waterways and a fundamental part of our waterway heritage. Strangely I have always felt sorry for those who boat there, I always feel they seem to have to fight for everything and yet these are the very custodians of our waterway heritage. I suppose the other big disadvantage is whenever you sail down the canal you've got to turn around and sail back! What more iconic place could there be than Shannon Harbour developed after 1800 as the terminus of the Grand Canal just before it terminates in the Shannon. I haven't seen it since Waterways Ireland modernised the place but I liked what I saw; floating history was everywhere and the gaunt shell of the old hotel where the crows, or were they jackdaws had taken over residency sent my imagination running riot. The harbourmaster's house built in 1806 and resplendent now as a bed and breakfast looks picture postcard like and the haunting desolate Royal Irish Constabulary Barracks conjured up thoughts of mustering famine victims aboard vessels with memories of loved ones etched in their brain and heading for a new and what they thought would be a better world.

It's a busy place Shannon Harbour, though sadly not as busy as it once was. There are two dry docks here, I suppose I was privileged to be able to wander (before health and safety issues went ballistic and, for me, spoiled my freedom) and I got to see the blocks the barges rested on, watched hulls being settled and steadied before sandblasting, welding and painting and got talking to people, those who shared my passion for old boats. The old

*Scherzer Bridge
on the North
Wall Quay*

overhead gantries demonstrated to me how the cargoes were unloaded before being stored in the shed, now we've got railings and locked gates and internet access ... oh dear, is this really progress? I'm not going to describe every feature from here to Dublin, buy the Grand Canal guide, but places like Rahan, Tullamore where Waterways Ireland have their workshops and are custodians of some old M boats, of the Kilbeggan line up to the restored canal stores, Daingean reformatory originally an army barracks then a reformatory (the very thought sends shivers down my spine) and now enjoying a more peaceful existence as a store for the National Museum of Ireland. I do know the local Offaly Historical Society has the reputation of being one of the most active in the country.

The Barrow line, Robertstown, and my favourite place called Prosperous lead us towards the Naas line and Sallins, Hazelhatch and the suburbs of Dublin. To think that anyone would have ever considered filling in the canal through Dublin is reprehensible yet it nearly happened! Thanks to our visionary founders it didn't happen. Grand Canal Dock and Ringsend Basin have been totally transformed by Dublin City Corporation and Waterways Ireland, now an area well apportioned it is perhaps for the well-heeled, the cafe culture has overtaken the former docklands and a beautiful yet underused marina is dominated by Bolands old mill. You must wander, see what remains of what was once three dry docks now reduced to two and perhaps if authority gets their way, there may be even one, have a look at the sea

Restaurant boat operating on the Grand Canal in Dublin

lock dropping boats into the tidal Liffey alongside the River Dodder.

Across the River and slightly to the left is Spencer Dock, a very different area now to what it was in its former glory days. On entering from the Liffey, the first view is of the massive Schertzer Bridge, although capable of being lifted, sadly they no longer operate; if they were to open, there would be traffic chaos on the Dublin quays! The Dock area is no more, in its place are modern office accommodation and restaurants one of which I found most interesting, a fascinating underground arched enclave where the stored bags of grain have given way to paninis, peppers and pasta – progress or simply change? It is still possible to moor bank-side here after that first lock, I find the Sheriff Street lifting bridge yet another fascinating piece of archaeological metal history, well worth a stare with a boyish wonder of just how it

works, sadly it too doesn't work anymore, perhaps someday, someone will catch the vision. Onwards then to what is now referred to as the Effin Bridge, formerly named the Newcomen Railway Lifting Bridge , a neglected and densely littered dirty area that could be made so much more attractive even with a simple clean up; enough criticism, onwards under the towering stand of Croke Park, I must confess I've only ever walked this stretch, pause for a seat beside Behan's bench where the infamous Brendan chats as only he could do, hasten as on the opposite bank tower the walls of Mountjoy Jail, quicken your step, eventually the impressive historic Glasnevin Cemetery can just about be seen. I'm tempted to continue but the fans of the Grand Canal would be jealous if I were to wax lyrical about the sites of the Royal while precluding their equally impressive canal.

I'm not a lover of modern architecture but I am inspired at Ireland's spaghetti junction where the canal, railway line and the Navan Road cross the M50 in company with a water main and an indistinguishable sewer pipe. Concrete over steel, grey, noisy and gaunt but functional, it all works and then a degree of peace as the waterway threads west firstly through what is known as the deep sinking. The Ryewater Aqueduct, Maynooth with St Patrick's College is a must see; all fall into the background as the canal goes really rural through the bog towards Mullingar, the home of the showband legend, Joe Dolan. I've sailed the last section with magical evocative names like Coolnahay, Ballynacargy, Abbeyshrule where the canal crosses the River Inny at the Whitworth Aqueduct and where from the landing strip I could fly home! Tagshinny, Ballymahon just escape being canal side as does the Corlea Bog Visitor Centre where an ancient oak trackway has been dated to 148 BC, look too for the bogman an impressive bog oak sculpture!

Foigha and Keenagh is where IWAI established the baby branch of the Association, no doubt one of their aims will be to promote the re-opening of the abandoned Longford Branch leading boat traffic up into Longford town. It's not far now to Cloondara and the beautifully restored Richmond Harbour. I'll never forget attending the celebration to re-open the canal in 2010 after 50 years of abandonment; John McKeown was the Waterways Ireland engineer who masterminded the project, conjure up the image as the Royal Canal Band played aboard 'Sakeena' as boats entered the basin and the proudest man to witness it all was Ian Bath, the visionary gentleman in the truest sense, who more than anyone inspired, cajoled and believed and delivered the project. Cloondara and Shannon Bridge boast examples of those idyllic lock-house cottages designed by Thomas Omer, the engineer who designed the Belfast to Sprucefield section of the Lagan Canal.

I've got to return to Lowtown on the Grand Canal to endeavour to describe Ireland's best-kept waterway secret, the Barrow navigation. I well recall some years ago launching small boats at Bagnelstown and cruising all the way to the tidal lock at St Mullins; it's not that I don't know the Northern section, but not every inch by boat. Athy is a bustling small town full of historical interest; from the town's bridge White's Castle is a picture postcard setting and beyond at Ardreigh Lock is the first of the very many ruined mills; this was a flour mill and was closed in the 1920s. The Barrow navigation is a series of canal cut and river sections, depth in the summer months can be a problem, I've always worked on the theory of having a boat with a two foot draught, to be sure, to be sure, to be sure; however local knowledge is best! Levitstown Mill, once a malting house sending the finished product to Guinness in Dublin is a very impressive structure; more castle-like than mill it stands gaunt beside the lock. More impressive buildings and more locks bring us to Carlow, the county town. Carlow is a very ancient settlement liberally endowed with fine architectural buildings though some in quite a derelict state; there is a very picturesque bridge dating back to 1569 and the remains of what once was a castle guarding the river and dating back to the 1180s.

The Barrow navigation boasts numerous examples of lifting bridges, basic but effectively designed and often user operated, but it is the old stone bridges that ooze history; the one at Leiglinbridge dates back to 1320, built by the Canon of Kildare Cathedral to facilitate movement throughout his diocese. I mentioned boating from Bagenalstown south, in fact I towed a boat all the way from the North only to discover the outboard engine

Fenniscourt Lock on the Barrow

wouldn't pump water and despite endless attempts, I couldn't get an impeller anywhere; mind you the engine had been serviced before leaving home but was tested with a hose and the pressure was sufficient to push water out through the exhaust. Thankfully a colleague gave me a lift so I didn't miss out the experience, sadly it rained and rained and rained and this supposedly was the sunny south-east! As we sailed alongside the grassy towpath, but on the Barrow it's not called a towpath, it's called the "Barrow Track" we came upon some fishermen; who should I recognise but a neighbour of mine, in fact a chap I used to teach with; just imagine going all that distance just to meet someone you'd seen the previous week!

Don't miss the views from high up the ravine overlooking Clashganna lock; this is an area of truly outstanding beauty, amazingly awesome and yet it gets better. Graiguenamanagh looms next, a settlement divided by the river where boats moor on both banks right beside the main street. I have friends whose boat was called Duiske, a boat that travelled the waterways of Ireland, I knew they were from this area but didn't know the boat was called after an old abbey, again a must see. More historical remains to be seen but soon St Mullins looms; it is here on the other side of the lock that the water becomes salty, the tidal section begins. The region is known as the area of the Three Sisters, being the river basins of the Barrow, Nore and Suir; perhaps the most atmospheric place for coffee is the Circle of Friends in Inistioge, coffee that hits the spot! Wander down to see the steamer

Red house on the Nore on a misty morning

hole, Inistioge is on the River Nore just before it joins the Barrow, this is where the film with the same name as the coffee shop was made and also that called Widow's Peak. The rivers Barrow, Nore and Suir all converge in the Waterford estuary. I've driven to Carrick-on-Suir, a delightful place with friendly people, went to see Portlaw, a Quaker village quite like Bessbrook in the north, Portlaw was built by the Malcolmson family to ensure their workers enjoyed good living conditions, I've marvelled at the stately homes of the area.

A little further east lies the Slaney River rising in the Wicklow Mountains tumbling down through Baltinglass, Tullow, Bunclody and to the limit of navigation, Enniscorthy before reaching the sea at Wexford also known as Loch Garman. Wexford is blessed with two harbours, an outer and an inner, one leading to the other via a narrow rocky channel. The tidal Slaney from Enniscorthy to the estuary is a slow meandering spread out river, teeming with wildlife and bordered on the west bank virtually all the way by the railway line and road. As the river slows there are shallows and mud flats, there is an area going up river beyond Killurin known as The Patches and they are just that, patches of mud, local guidance or a copy of Cecil G Miller's book is necessary to successfully navigate this area; going up stream there is a landmark called The Boiler, I gather this is the boiler from an old steam trading boat which was thrown to the east bank as the result of an explosion. I well remember attending a Slaney Branch picnic at Killurin Pier, a delightful grassy bank side area where there is a seat erected in memory of two Slaney stalwarts, Cecil Miller and Paddy Hatton.

My last area to comment on is without doubt one of the prettiest and dramatic of all navigations, The Corrib nestling in Connemara; this is *Quiet Man* country. I never cease to be amazed at the popularity of this film; even today, sixty-two years since its release, it is still possible to buy a copy! The lake is managed by the Corrib Trustees, the River Corrib connects the lake to Galway City, and indeed I know many will have stood on the bridge watching the salmon leap as the fresh water tumbles towards the sea. The short Eglington Canal once linked the River Corrib to the sea and around the same era construction began of the Cong Canal to link Lough Corrib to Lough Mask, but construction was eventually abandoned. On my trip it rained and rained and rained, boats were launched close to Cong and all participants had a look at Ashford Castle from the lake, always an awesome sight. My late father visited here in the 1950s and was so impressed he returned home and called our house "Ashford". The plan was to head across the lake to Maam Bridge, my what an awesome trip, I'll never forget the towering mountains looming down, the lively waters and the final trip down the Bealnabrack River to Keane's Pub for a very welcome hot lunch. Like the Erne the Corrib is reputed to have three hundred and sixty five islands, I really wonder if anyone has ever bothered to count them or is it just like many large houses that are reputed to have that number of windows! Further essential reading must be Wilde's *Lough Corrib* written by Oscar Wilde's father William, who had a summer residence by the lake or from three quite elusive books written by Maurice Semple, *Some Galway Memories, Reflections on Lough Corrib* and *By the Corribside*.

Ashford Castle Hotel

Ram's Island

Ram's Island is the largest island on Lough Neagh, being nearly one mile long by a quarter of a mile wide at the widest southern end. The Lough Neagh drainage scheme of the mid 1800s created a water-line stone revetment, which was being removed by visitors; this is a very rare example marking the natural shoreline of Lough Neagh as most other natural shoreline marks around Lough Neagh have disappeared.

In 2005 Lord O'Neill granted RBLNA [River Bann and Lough Neagh Association] a 30-year lease for Ram's Island and a similar 30-year lease from the Earl of Shaftesbury for the ground the jetty is built on. After taking advice it was decided to form a non-profit making limited company to take the project forward and to take on the leases for the Island. The new company called the River Bann and Lough Neagh Association Company was incorporated in January 2005, the Company achieved Charitable Status in 2007.

A sub-committee was formed from members and stakeholders to take the project forward and they began to identify the elements of the project. These are the main elements.

Interpretive Facilities

Ram's Island and the Lough Neagh wetlands have a lot to offer the visitor in terms of natural and built history. It was originally thought to provide an interpretive centre on the Island to educate visitors but following discussions with NIEA, our own research and because of possible environmental impacts and prohibitive costs it was decided to use a floating facility aboard a barge moored at the Island during the visitor season. The barge (JK 16) an ex John Kelly coal lighter was originally used to transport coal along the Lagan from the Belfast coal quays to the gasworks in Belfast. It was donated to the Ram's Island Heritage Project by Readymix Ltd.

The Ferry Boat Project Element

This was the culmination of a lot of hard work by all concerned with the Ram's Island Project. We had attended numerous meetings with funders and other stake holders, drew up a detailed spec of what was needed for the job and went through a tendering process. We acknowledge the generosity of our funders, **Antrim Borough Council, Department of Agriculture and Rural**

Development, Department of Culture Arts and Leisure, Ulster Garden Villages Limited and last but not least the Lough Neagh Partnership. We would also like to thank all the volunteer members who visited Scotland to view the vessel and to help bring her home, at their own expense I might add. The provision of the ferry-boat for Ram's Island has helped bring the project to life, helped us to attain our goals for the Island and make the Island available to all. Although her primary purpose is ferrying visitors to Ram's Island, the "Island Warrior" is available for charter anywhere on the Lough Neagh system. In 2012 the "Island Warrior" carried the Olympic Flame across Lough Neagh.

The New Jetty

In 2005 access to the island was difficult as the jetty, built in the sixties, had fallen into disrepair. The old jetty had been repaired with volunteers but we wanted to build a new structure to assist better access to the Island for boaters, visitors and the general public. We believed that the creation of another Island Destination on Lough Neagh would benefit the whole of the Lough Neagh Wetlands. After costing the new jetty with contractors the funders told us they could only provide £100,000 to build a new jetty and the cheapest contractor was £170,000. After discussions with DARD and the Lough Neagh Partnership, it was decided to build the new jetty with volunteers and the funders providing funds to buy materials and equipment, the only stipulation was the work was to be overseen by a qualified engineer. It took a long time to construct the jetty, over two years but we now have the best jetty on Lough Neagh. We also have the necessary equipment on the Island to be used as various maintenance jobs arise.

Volunteers and Visitors

Last year we had over eight thousand visitors and volunteers on Ram's Island (including members from other branches) and hope that figure will increase this year. We usually kick off the year by celebrating World Wetlands Day on the Island with a public volunteer litter lift and tour of the Island. World Wetlands Day is on the 2nd of February each year and celebrates the Convention on Wetlands of International Importance, called the Ramsar Convention; it is an intergovernmental treaty that provides the framework for national action and international co-operation for the conservation and wise use of wetlands and their resources. The Ramsar Convention is the only global environmental treaty that deals with a particular ecosystem. The treaty was adopted in the Iranian city of Ramsar in 1971 and the Convention's member countries cover all geographic regions of the planet. The Convention's mission is "the conservation and wise use of all wetlands through local and national actions and international cooperation, as a contribution towards achieving sustainable development throughout the world". Lough Neagh and of course Ram's Island are a designated Ramsar Site.

The Future

Antrim Borough Council has supported us with running costs from the start of the project and hopefully will continue to do so. We have raised and spent in excess of £300,000 for the capital projects. Amongst the many things on the agenda for the future are the improvement of the new jetty, the upgrading of the path network, tree surgery, the restoration of the O'Neill cottage, a properly conducted archaeological dig and more definitive interpretive signage. Invasive species removal will naturally continue.

Our Volunteers are like gold dust to the project.

Michael Savage.

Top right; The ferry boat, "The Island Warrior"

Bottom right; The new jetty.

Bottom left; Ruins of the O'Neill summer house with the round tower in the background.

Working party ready to go

A Brief History of the IWAI

The Early Years Of IWAI

Early in 1952, with the success of the IWA in England and the publication of Harry Rice's book, *Thanks for the Memory* concern was being expressed about the proposed replacement of the opening span in the bridge at Athlone (it had been a swing bridge) and how such a decision could influence developments at Roosky and Tarmonbarry.

The issue of replacing the Athlone Bridge with a fixed span was because although the airdraft here would be reasonable, it would create a precedent and some of the other opening bridges on the river would be too low for a fixed span. The situation was ultimately solved when CIE placed two passenger boats on the river, which required sufficiently high headroom to cater for existing boats but in future it would exclude all sailing boats with masts.

Also in 1952, enthusiasts had published a number of articles and letters in the *Irish Times* highlighting how detrimental such obstructions could decimate the future leisure use of the waterway. Commercial boating on the Shannon was in decline, rail and road transport had dealt a death blow to waterway transportation and while some commercial boating activity struggled on into the

Athlone Bridge

1960s, many of the boats were being sold off, converted to sand barges and even for conversion to house and leisure boats. Thankfully many survived and as a result of the dreams and visions of a few, we have today many examples of new life being breathed into the ghosts of the past, and still plying our sweet waters.

I can do no better than quote from the chronology on the IWAI web site of that early meeting;

December, 1953 Meeting held at 58 Seafield Road. Decision to form an Irish I.W.A. and send out notices calling an inaugural A.G.M, to elect officers. This notice was signed by Harry Rice, Vincent Delany. Alf Delany, Bunny Goodbody, Walter Levinge and Rory O'Hanlon.

*07-Jan-54   Inaugural meeting held
in Shelbourne Hotel attended by over 200
people. The following officers and mem-
bers of Council were elected: President,
Colonel H. J. Rice; Vice-Presidents, Major
General H, MacNeill, Prof. J. Johnston,
Prof. J. Henry. T. G. Wilson, S. MacBride,
P. J. Lenihan, J. J. O'Leary, J. F. McCormick,
G. Shackleton, D. Williams, W. Levinge and
A. Turney; Hon. Secretaries, Vincent Delany
and L. M. Goodbody. Hon. Treasurer,
G.C.M. Thompson. Council. Dr. R. O'Hanlon,
Dr. A. Delany. Major E. H. Waller. Frank Waters.
Dr. J, de Courcy, Ireland, D. Kearns, S. Hooper,
Dr. P. C. Denham. A. B. Killeen and S. Shine.*

*1954   The following resolution was passed unani-
mously: "That this Association is resolutely opposed
to any attempt to amend the Shannon Navigation
Acts so as to permit the obstruction of the Shannon
Navigation and, in particular, its obstruction
by the erection of a fixed bridge at Athlone."*

The vision of these passionate pioneers established the foundations of our Association and on
the 19th February 1954, the Athlone Branch was
formed. Success was swift for the fledgling group;
in June that year plans by CIE for Athlone Bridge
were withdrawn as were the proposed restrictions
at Roosky and Tarmonbarry. The success was infectious, for the next year saw branches established
at Killaloe, Nenagh, Carlow on the Barrow navigation and Mullingar on the Royal Canal.

Who then were these visionaries, the forefathers
of our Association? Colonel Harry Rice is perhaps
best known for his book, *Thanks for the Memory*
the story of the mighty River Shannon and for
the associated charts he produced. It is fair to
state Harry with the Delanys were the fundamental driving force behind the establishment of the
Association we all revere. Harry owned Dunrovin,
that beautiful, quaint tin roofed cottage at Coosan
on the shores of Lough Ree eventually bequeathed
to the Association. Harry with his first wife Peggy
were familiar faces cruising Lough Ree and the
River in their open boat. *Thanks for the Memory*
was the result of a seven-year labour of love, it endeavoured to chart and mark Lough Ree for leisure use, a navigation known intimately by the
commercial boatmen who had sailed the waters
from Dublin to Killaloe and North into Lough
Allen and Lough Key.

Harry Rice was born in Portarlington in 1894
and was educated at Portora Royal School in
Enniskillen and his third level education was received at Trinity College, Dublin. He qualified as
a medical doctor and served with the British Army
in the Royal Medical Corps seeing service during
the First World War, and after a short career as
Port Embarkation Officer in Brussels served for a
further twenty five years in the Indian Army.

In 1922 Harry married an Athlone girl, Peggy,
someone he described as his "companion in adventure" sadly Peggy never saw the publication of
the book of which she was so much an essential

element, as she passed away in 1951, the book was first published in 1952. Harry's second wife was called Cynthia; many will recall this delightful lady who also became synonymous with a passion for the waterways and the Athlone Branch. Such was the success of the book it has been reprinted on two subsequent occasions. Harry's charts published in 1960 are now in the care of the Heritage Boat Association. Sadly Harry passed away in 1964, the same year as his colleague and co-founder of IWAI, Vincent Delany; what a tragic loss to this fledgling group, yet the success already achieved would ensure the Association would flourish and mature to become the respected voice of the waterways.

The name of Delany is synonymous with the early success of IWAI. Dr Vincent Delany was described as "The Master of the Upper North Shannon" he was a man with a tremendous local knowledge, something he passed on to his two sons. Professor Vincent T H Delany was a prominent Dublin lawyer who had written a very powerful article (published in the *Irish Times*) towards the end of 1951which articulated the neglect of our waterways, a resource he asserted could be further enhanced to sustain commercial activity and an even greater attribute was the development of tourism and wider leisure use. Vincent's brother Dr Alfred F Delany more commonly known as Alf or, to his close friends, Pompey; Vincent was the husband of Ruth, both husband and wife played a pivotal role in the establishment of the fledgling Association.

Mr Sean McBride was the influential politician who gave support to the organisation and who ensured the "message" was heard in the right places. The only child of Maud Gonne and Major John McBride, Sean was born in Paris and moved to Ireland when he was thirteen; he always spoke with a pronounced French accent. Sean was a dedicated Republican; as well as being a government minister and noted barrister, Sean was a prominent international politician, and a recipient of both the Nobel and Lenin Peace prizes for his work with Amnesty International. He was a tremendous supporter of the Shannon system and played a pivotal role in political influence on matters, which would have had a detrimental effect on the navigation. At the inaugural Athlone Branch meeting he proposed "that the meeting views with alarm the condition of the Clarendon Lock at Knockvicar and urges in the national interest that immediate repairs be carried out"; the result was that the lock was repaired and re-opened in 1956. Sean was a close friend of Harry Rice; I must admit I smile when I think of a dedicated Republican being best friends with a retired Colonel of the British Army; well it is Ireland and let's face it, just about anything can happen here!

Mr Llewellyn M Goodbody, affectionately known as Bunny, was the enthuastistic boater of the group. Bunny had bought the "Phoenix" in 1950, a steam yacht with what can only be described as a 'distinguished' history. Bunny Goodbody had lived initially on the boat in Dromineer before moving into Waterloo Lodge at Kilgarvan. While

M Y Phoenix in Connaught Harbour, Portumna 1952

researching for this book, I'd a lovely letter from Reggie Goodbody, which describes the above much better than I can.

"In 1949 my father bought the "Phoenix", did some conversion, and the family then lived on her for two and a half years in Dromineer, a delightful life for a small boy. In the winter she was moved in under the roof of the old canal store basin, which still exists, and there I spent some very cold and damp nights. (There was no heating in the aft cabin, and the decks leaked, which meant hanging half a tent over my bunk.) Two of the local houses drew their water from the corner of the basin in two metal pipes. (They are still there). A local politician saw an opportunity to garner a few votes in Dromineer, as he said the "Phoenix" was polluting the water in the basin, which we were. He then proposed that a council by-law would be introduced prohibiting any house boat from mooring within

100 yards of the Tipperary shore Fortunately this was never enacted but it raised alarm bells with the boating community, and was one of the reasons why the Inland Waterways Association was formed. I think my father L M Goodbody (but known as Bunny), & Vincent Delany were the first joint secretaries of the Association. When we visited Lough Ree for the 1952 regatta, the "Phoenix" stayed on for the summer, and my parents were very friendly with Harry Rice who was a frequent visitor aboard the "Phoenix", and also on occasion Sean McBride. Harry Rice was doing his surveys for *Thanks for the Memory*. During the 1960s I was friendly with the Denham family, and I can clearly remember the enormous amount of time Peter Denham, who was then secretary of the IWAI, spent fighting to save the circle line of the Grand Canal. The Dublin Corporation had the brilliant idea of building a sewer under the canal and then a road on top, but fortunately they did not get away with it. In my opinion stopping this was one of the most important things the association did, as otherwise the Grand Canal would have died, all the way to the Shannon, and probably the Royal as well, and we would have lost a large amount of our waterways heritage".

Dr Peter C Denham was the first honorary secretary of the Association; isn't it interesting to note the proliferation of medical personnel in the early days of the Association, another, Rory O'Hanlon was a gynaecologist who lived with his wife Barbara in Clonskeagh, Dublin. Peter Denham often sailed dragon class sailing boats, they were brought by rail from Dublin and launched at Banagher, they sailed the Shannon and often raced out of Dromineer.

Walter Levinge came from a truly waterway enthuastist family, his father Mr D R Levinge, although latterly crippled with arthritis for many years, sailed the waters of Killenure, Coosan and Lough Ree. He lived at Creaghduff House near the shores of Coosan Lough. Walter, his son spent his early years in Canada where he learnt the craft of boat building, locals will still testify to the skill of this master boat builder. Walter knew the Lough intimately and had a vast knowledge of sailing skills and of navigation. In his eighty odd years he vividly recalled the change in the boats that sailed the lake, from the big forty ton yachts such as the "Island Queen" and the "Countess" to the wooden sailing trading barges commonly known as turf boats, the last of which, the Sand Lark ended her life after a fire at Garrykennedy. Eventually the steamboat gave way to the boat powered by a petrol/paraffin engine and laterally the proliferation of outboard powered craft. Sadly Walter passed away in October 1982.

The influence of Rolt's *Green and Silver*, the correspondence in the *Irish Times* and local newspapers cannot be underestimated, these really fired interest and enthusiasm and the newly formed organisation literally hit the ground running. While the Association was based on the newly formed IWA in England it very soon adopted its own personality being driven by personalities and unique Irish challenges. It was natural the struggle should move to Athlone where the old swivel bridge required replacement. The first Chair of the Athlone Branch was Mr W A Tormey, he and the other officers with the committee faced an uphill struggle as public opinion seemed to favour the less expensive solution, placing a concrete structure at parapet level which would result in considerably less headroom. With sheer persistency the branch managed to curry support from the local press,

The "St Ciaran" scrapes under a Barrow bridge.

the Westmeath Independent, and the catastrophe of having fixed bridges was eventually averted. The additional headroom was required for the soon to be acquired CIE passenger boats which would ply the Shannon as passenger cruisers. The battle was never easy and necessitated tremendous determination. This struggle established the new group as the "voice of the waterways" something the Association still aspires to achieve.

Colonel Rice and Sean McBride TD organised a boat trip on John William's boat the "St Clair" in August of 1954. John Williams was Harry Rice's son-in-law, married to Betty, Harry's daughter. On board were the Tanaiste, William Norton and the Chairman of CIE, Ted Courtney; this persuaded CIE to purchase two passenger cruisers, the "St Brendan" to be based in Athlone and the "St Ciaran" based in Ballina/Killaloe. The newly formed Athlone branch organised a group of local boaters to welcome the "St Brendan" to Athlone where she was to be berthed. The boats were acquired on the Norfolk Broads and operated relatively successfully for just short of twenty years, eventually being sold to the Galley restaurant business in New Ross where they operated as restaurant boats and where they are still berthed; currently the "St Ciaran" still operates for river dining cruises. In 1955 branches were formed at Killaloe and at Nenagh, while a branch on the Royal was formed at Mullingar and at Carlow on the Barrow navigation.

Over the years many small rallies were organised but 1961 saw the first of the really big boat rallies, pleasure boats of all shapes and sizes assembled below the bridge in Athlone en route for Lough Key. Seventy-one boats took part and the fuel for the engines was supplied free of charge by Esso. This was a weeklong event; one of the highlights being the dinner dance on board the CIE cruiser "St Ciaran" on the August Bank Holiday Monday, the cruiser sailed south and didn't return to the quayside until 2.30am, no wonder Tuesday was a free day for all participants!

Of course the Association is about much more than the Shannon navigation; in 1963 the circular line of the Grand Canal in Dublin was in threat of closure as Dublin Corporation had plans to install a sewer in the bed of the Grand Canal, concreting it over and creating a high speed road link on the surface; thankfully those in authority listened to the voice of the City Hall protesters and the canal was saved. 1964 saw the formation of the Dublin Branch and the subsequent years saw the branch actively organise work parties, boat rallies and constantly lobby the City Council to ensure a future for one of the city's finest assets. It is fair to say those on the North side of Dublin became concerned at so much interest being taken in the protection of the Grand while the Royal Canal seemed to be overlooked. Under the auspices of the IWAI the Royal Canal Amenity Group was founded in April of 1974 by Dr Ian Bath and while an independent organisation with separate branches along the Royal it worked very much in partnership with IWAI.

Interest and life was certainly becoming alive on our lakes, rivers and canals, the spring of 1962 saw the first Barrow Boat Rally highlighting this amazing waterway and all it had to offer. Leisure boating on the Erne became more organised with the Belturbet Branch being established in 1964 with the first Lough Erne Rally being organised in 1967, while the Lough Erne Branch was established some twelve years later in 1979. A second Northern Branch was established at Scarva on the Newry Canal in 1980 and was enthusiastically lobbying for the re-opening of the Newry Canal. On 26th September 1987, the Scarva Branch organised a very successful boat rally in conjunction with the Newry Canal Preservation Society through the Victoria Lock on the Newry Ship Canal.

Controversy abounded regarding the future of the Royal canal, it was arranged that the Grand Canal would be transferred from CIE to OPW but the important issue was to ensure the Royal Canal would also be transferred, otherwise CIE would have continued to neglect it. Many thought CIE had become disinterested in the canals and indeed would have been happy to oversee their demise.

Our south-eastern boaters organised the Slaney Branch at Wexford Boat Club in 1989 to promote boating on the navigable Slaney from Wexford up to Enniscorthy, while the Corrib Branch was established in 1958 to promote that much under-valued Lakeland paradise. The River Bann and Lough Neagh Association was established as a standalone organization in 1967 and successfully lobbied to maintain the Lower Bann as a navigable waterway; they affiliated as a Branch of IWAI in 1998.

The IWAI trailer "selling the vision"

The Association Today

Today the Association is a limited company with charitable status registered in the Republic; moves are afoot to register the company in Northern Ireland and to seek charitable status. This will enable the Association to reclaim income tax paid by the member on each subscription. The Association is governed by Articles of Association and currently there are twenty-one branches, two of which are special interest groups, the remainder are navigation based. Virtually all areas of the country are covered and like the water that freely flows in our rivers and lakes, we recognise no political boundaries, being an all island organization.

The Association elects a President who generally serves for a three year term and who is responsible for the day-to-day running of the Association. That

Dunrovin

person would have served their apprenticeship as Vice President and their knowledge isn't lost as they serve a further three years as Past President. The Executive Board of Directors presents itself annually for election and meets monthly to administer policy decisions generally set by the Council who meet three times a year. The Council is made up of two representatives of every branch, one of which must be an office bearer, members of the Executive and six elected members chosen at the Annual General Meeting.

At National level, the Executive of the Association meets at least once a year with the senior management team of Waterways Ireland to liaise on national issues; relevant meetings are also arranged with the two Departments and with the two Ministers and periodically the North South Ministerial Council.

In the North the Association has representatives on the Lagan Canal Trust, the Ulster Canal steering group run under the auspices of the Blackwater Regional Partnership. We have also representation on the Lough Neagh Partnership. The River Bann and Lough Neagh Association have formed an independent company with Directors to administer the Ram's Island project, an island on Lough Neagh leased from Lord O'Neill while the Newry/Portadown Branch has representation on the Joint Council committee, which administers any development relevant to the Newry Canal.

The late Harry Rice had a waterside property at Coosan Point; known affectionately as "Dunrovin", it was located on the southern shores of Lough Ree at Killinure Point. His widow Cynthia, nee McWeeney, bequeathed the property in August 1997 to the Inland Waterways Association in the trust of the Athlone Branch. Cynthia's bequest stated the property should be "used in perpetuity as a Clubhouse/Meeting House for members"; she further stated "as many of the existing trees thereon shall be retained". The property is an old Nissan hut with the roof concreted over and is now in poor condition; there are other associated smaller buildings all standing on a site of approximately one acre. If you've never been to Dunrovin; please go, see and witness the idyllic beauty of this enchanting place.

The Association organizes a number of major boat rallies each year, the Shannon Boat Rally, the Erne Boat Rally, Lough Derg Rally, Shannon Harbour, Dublin Rally and the Lough Neagh rally; the biggest would be the Shannon Rally jointly organised by a committee made up from Athlone and Carrick on Shannon Branches. The Erne Boat Rally is organised by a committee formed by representatives of the Belturbet and Lough Erne Branches while the Lough Derg rally is organized by a sub-committee of Lough Derg Branch. Shannon Harbour Branch organise a static boat rally annually at Shannon Harbour while many of the canal branches combine to organise canal rallies as do the Barrow branches. Each year Dublin Branch organizes a trip into the city; this is an important event ensuring canal traffic is kept alive. For the last few years Offaly Branch have successfully organised 'Float to the Fleadh' in Tullamore on the Grand Canal; Corrib and other branches also organise rallies and cruise in company events.

Sadly other than the Erne, the Lower Bann and Lough Neagh many of the Northern navigations are currently classified as abandoned waterways; not to be outdone local branches have organized events on the Lagan, the Newry, Coalisland and Ulster Canals as well as the Upper Bann. Hence the Northern Branches see themselves in more of a campaigning mode always required to sell their dream product to politicians and civil servants, urging them to "catch the vision". The re-opening of the Ulster Canal which links Lough Neagh with Lough Erne remains our major project; we see this as "The Missing Link" in the waterway chain allowing navigation from Coleraine in the North to Limerick in the West, Dublin in the East and Waterford in the South. While it is encouraging to see the first phase now through planning, we await developments regarding finance.

Sometimes I feel the Southern Canal Branches feel overshadowed by the Shannon yet it is fair to say they have achieved so much in their own

The recently restored Richmond Harbour

quiet way. Here the struggle is by no means over, The Longford line of the Royal Canal and the Kilbeggan branch of the Grand Canal are two projects which must not be forgotten and access to Dublin must be promoted. One of our hidden secrets is without doubt the Breffni Erne waterway, from Belturbet up to Lough Oughter in the Cavan lake lands, yet despite a grandiose launch attended by supportive politicians, no progress to date has been achieved. I well realise this is very much an environmentally sensitive area but that should not preclude efforts to open up this region and expose its beauty; here also is the possibility of a link to Garadice Lake on the Shannon Erne waterway creating an amazing scenic circular loop.

Is today's Association fit for purpose? Well I think so; in fact I feel the present leadership offered by both our President and Vice President is exemplary. It's easy to criticise; I've read hurtful things regarding past decisions of our Association written by those who obviously hadn't all the facts. It is true some years ago the Association over two working days looked at current practice and made recommendations as to how it was felt the Association should change; largely those recommendations were implemented. Sadly membership has fallen over recent years but that is common in many other organisations, it is due to the drastic downturn in our economy, put simply, folk now think seriously how they spend their money, and let's face it, membership of an Association is not essential spending!

Our website, manned by volunteers, is constantly being updated and is hugely popular, often an embarrassment to others! It is true we embarked on a procedure to examine if we should appoint a paid employee, yes we took our time but we brought the membership with us; sadly we lost the services of an excellent employee because we just couldn't afford the cost; the budget set was far exceeded by expenditure and a difficult decision had to be taken. The latest challenge is the threat of increased charging on the canals no doubt to be followed by a similar scheme for the rest of the system; if these plans are based on the English model of raising revenue it will fail. Why? Because we just don't have the population base with sufficient financial resources in Ireland to sustain such demands. I've often heard it said; you can gently lead the Irish people, but you can't push them; perhaps this lesson needs to be relearnt! Recently the Association has moved to an online membership system; quite simply if it wasn't for the time generosity of one of our members, we just couldn't have afforded it.

Where To Now?

Sometimes we need to look back in order to see the way forward; questions that spring to mind for the future of the Association are; is the future of the navigation safe, are we confident it is in good hands; is the battle won; is the Association fit for purpose; what are the threats we need to address, what is the future for abandoned navigations, is our waterway heritage protected?

A seal makes its way up the Slaney

At the time of writing there is real concern over the future regulation of the Grand, Royal and Barrow navigations. These are fragile waterway economies, they are underused yet they offer some of the most amazing scenery and potential cruising and walking experience of any waterways in Ireland. There is no doubt that a problem exists regarding regulation and implementation of existing bylaws but I'm not sure over-regulation and higher charges are the answer to the problem, in fact I'm convinced they are not. Personally I'd like to see these navigations properly marketed, that certainly has not been done effectively, infrastructure is needed, marinas and hire cruisers and facilities for tourists. I know we haven't the weather but we have so much more to offer in niche tourism, fishing, walking, cruising, the list is endless and let's not forget the awesome Irish hospitality. I can hear already the comments of those in author-

ity, boaters need to pay for facilities provided; fine but get the user base up first, just be careful you don't already kill off what is a fragile system. The future is not all about boaters or boating, it's as much about all who use the towpath, about bringing life to the waterway

In the Republic the Royal Canal needs to be completed, the Longford Branch lies waiting, on the Grand Canal the Kilbeggan Branch has taken its place in the line; there are numerous other projects and don't let's forget the Corrib, the Slaney and smaller navigations such as the Suir. In the North the problem is huge; gracious where do we start as most of the navigations have been abandoned; well the obvious is to reinstate the "Missing Link" in our waterway chain; the Ulster Canal, a waterway that completes the picture joining Lough Neagh with Lough Erne, a waterway that when reinstated will create a cruising ground enviable of any in Western Europe! I state the obvious when I say the Ulster must come first; it needs to be reopened to the same specifications as the Shannon Erne waterway, and then let's have the Lagan, the Newry and the short Coalisland canal, and don't forget the Strabane Canal restored but unused, take your pick which comes first. I know it's all to do with money, but these projects are labour intensive, they create jobs, when finished they augment Ireland's finest and possibly only growth industry; tourism. What we do not need is over regulation, that's happened in England, especially on the Thames, we need a sensible approach and freedom to enjoy this amazing resource that can't be bottled and sadly what has really been lacking to date; we need enlightened politicians with a vision!

Waterways are not just for boaters; the aim in developing this amazing resource is to get people; be they locals or visitors out into the great outdoors; to relax and enjoy fresh air and nature, to improve the health of the nation; the boat is the catalyst; that which brings life to the system.

The Shannon-Erne

Lobbying and work parties in the 1980's and 90's were dominated by the project to re-open the Shannon Erne waterway, formerly known as the Ballinamore/Ballyconnell canal. Originally this canal was the mother of all fiascos, it is said only nine boats were successful in navigating the original waterway, what a contrast to the phenomenal success of the re-opened canal. I recall the legendary John Weaving bringing his barge and dog to Leitrim and working tirelessly to clear vegetation as far as the first lock. Past President Liam D'Arcy brought the message to enthuse local branches and encourage lobbying of local politicians. Eventually the Taoiseach, Charles Haughey announced agreement from the two governments and on the back of a successful feasibility study carried out by the International Fund for Ireland, the cross border flagship project was agreed. The project was commenced in 1990 and took four years to complete utilising the Woodford River and navigating through St John's Lough, Lough Scur and the beautiful Garadice Lough.

Ironically the success of the original canal depended on the refurbishment of the neglected Ulster Canal, today the shoe is on the other foot; the Ulster Canal will bring enhanced success to the Shannon Erne.

With every good story there is always a 'but'; sadly ours is perhaps our biggest undertaking to date, the project to re-open the Ulster Canal, forty-six miles of abandoned waterway that once completed the waterway chain allowing navigation from Coleraine in the north to Limerick, Dublin and Waterford. We have coined the phrase "The Missing Link" yet despite over twenty odd years of lobbying the extensive plans to re-open the first phase as far as Clones are still a dream; no sod has yet been turned in this project that would revitalise this neglected cross border area. Ministerial meetings North and South continue, lobbying continues unabated, we need a political champion and to date none has had the courage to step forward. Who knows who yet may be challenged and might step up to the mark?

Bridge 8 at Kilclare, the Leitrim end of the canal

At the Erne end of the navigation; this is the Woodford River

*Ruth Delany and Dr Ian Bath chat to Albert Reynolds
at the re opening ceremony of the Royal Canal*

Some Special People!

Without doubt our Association has been enriched over the years by the special people that have given so generously of their time for the love of the Irish Waterways and the individual branches of our Association. Perhaps what I've tried to do over the following pages is risky; I'm bound to leave somebody out and I'm sure I have; apologies, I'm only human but these are folk that I knew, and know of; those who helped me compile the book said we've got to include details about so and so. I wanted to record details on those outstanding individuals who presently serve, on those who have been called to their heavenly home, details about very special people, some who never served as branch officers, some who were 'hands on' folk, perhaps not given to use of the pen but had so many qualities in so many other ways; I hope you knew some of these special people, if you didn't then like me; you are the poorer for missing out.

Dr Peter Denham

recalled by Brian Denham

I was 6 years old (1949) when my father first took me on a Shannon Holiday, camping from two collapsible canoes transported by train. He and my mother had done this before and the canoes had small sails to assist them across the lakes,

Dr Peter Denham

and no internal buoyancy nor were life jackets to be found! A year or so later we graduated to the "Betwixt" a converted ship's lifeboat owned by Val Landon of the Banagher Pottery. When some county councils planned low fixed bridges across the Upper Shannon, The Inland Waterways Association was formed and Peter volunteered as Secretary. Most of the early meetings were held in our home; when I came downstairs in the morning I would always know that there had been a meeting the night before because the place smelt like a pub and there would be a large number of empty Guinness bottles lying around!

Peter's chosen media to oppose low bridges and later to retain the circular line of the Grand Canal through Dublin was the letters' page of the *Irish Times* and the *Independent*. He wrote endless-

MY Phoenix in Killgarvan

ly both in a personal capacity and on behalf of the association seeking publicity for the marvelous potential of the river, objecting to bridges, closures, low slung power or telephone lines and so on. Nowadays it is hard to believe that such a wonderful tourism and recreational facility could have been under threat from Council managers, but in those early years recreational boating was regarded as an elitist activity. His stories of canoes and camping helped to dispel this notion. Fortunately there remained a small amount of commercial Barge Traffic between Guinness Brewery and Killaloe so the lower Shannon was not at the time threatened. Then my father (with his friend Peter Dobbs) purchased the "Charles Whitton" a former RNLI Lifeboat that had been based at Clogher head in Co Louth and built between 1880 & 1890 originally with oars and sails, later converted to petrol. It had a very shallow draft, less than two feet so we were able to explore every nook and cranny of the Shannon's inlets and tributaries.

We bathed by swimming in the river; Peter never wore togs and frequently would not bother to dress afterwards unless we were approaching a town. When he finally stood down as Secretary of the IWAI, the Association presented him with a watercolour of the "Charles Whitton".

A key event in the protection of the Navigation in the early years was getting Board Failte on the Association's side with a vision of the tourism potential; this occurred through personal contacts and shared adventures on the river, Douglas Heard with Ruth Delany and her professorial husband Vincent and brother-in-law Alf, Rory and Barbara O'Hanlon and many others all come to mind.

It probably helped that in those early years my mother's best friend from childhood was Betty Goodbody who was for some time living with her family on the "Phoenix" tied up at Goose Island in Dromineer, not a very comfortable existence and fortunately one that did not last too long. I stayed with them one summer holiday and made friends with Reggie, I cannot remember which year. The two Peters (Denham and Dobbs) converted the "Charles Whitton" back to sail, which was always used on lake crossings, although with her shallow draft she could not beat against the wind. There was discussion about restoring the twin centre-boards (Fore and Aft), which had been in place when she was originally launched as a lifeboat, but they would have occupied most of the cabin space so my mother quickly put a lid on those plans.

Dr. Michael Farrell

recalled by

Dr. Michael Farrell or "Doc" was born in Bagenalstown Co. Carlow and qualified in Medicine in RCSI in the early 1940's. After internship he joined The Royal Naval Volunteer reserve and soon saw action in the English Channel as ships' surgeon on board RNVR Monowai, assisting casualties extracted from the Normandy landings in 1944. Later, after the allied invasion of Europe was underway he was posted to Singapore to act as Port Medical Officer following the Japanese surrender. Returning to Ireland he undertook post graduate study in Public Health and following appointments in Kilkenny and Kerry, he was posted to Leitrim where he was to remain for the rest of his life. For some, a posting to Leitrim in the 1950's with its declining population, poor roads and absence of industry might have been seen as akin to a posting to the Russian Tundra. However he, along with several pals most notably Bill Child, Tom Maher, Brendan Lynch and Sean Hanahoe but including many other Carrick-on-Shannon stalwarts recognised the potential of the Shannon for leisure and tourism. A local branch of the newly formed IWAI was soon established. Meetings were held on a regular basis in The Bush Hotel. Rallies were planned.

An early workparty on the Shannon-Erne at Leitrim

The potential of a re-opened Ballinamore–Ballyconnell canal was not appreciated until many years later because the burning issue of the late 50's and early 60's was to restore the Knockvicar Lock entrance to Lough Key, which was duly accomplished. Among the earliest boat hire companies attracted to Carrick was Mitchel Marine run by Cliff & Gill Hogg who were prominent in the local IWAI. For several years "Doc" served as Able Seaman on board "Sampan" under the command of Bill Child. The two would disappear each year for The Rally – efforts to contact either were fruitless. No cell phones. The Doc's ever patient wife Mary would trawl the length of the Shannon with culinary delights for the two wandering sailors, usually to no avail. A few years later when The Doc commanded his own vessel – a Freeman 22 named "Monowai", Mary managed to leave some delicious lamb chops on board. Unfortunately, rather than putting the chops into the rudimentary fridge, Doc placed the lamb chops in a locker to-gether with his Rally closing dinner "good clothes" where all were discovered several days later, after a neighbouring rallier complained of the odour emanating from "Monowai". The years went quickly by and unfortunately the Doc had died before the B&B canal was officially re-opened in 1994 as the Shannon-Erne Waterway. Devoted to the Shannon, one of Doc's favourite pastimes was to sit in Dromod Harbour on a summer's evening looking out at the broad expanse of Lough Bofin and especially at the many boats which decided to cut inside the black mark located at the southern tip of Derrycarne. His love of the Shannon continues in the lives of his 3 children – Michael ["Lady Kate"], Anne Marie Brody ["Scavenger"], Gillian Daly ["Chiff-Chaff"] and his many grand-children who are regular visitors to the Shannon in general, and Carrick in particular.

Sean Fitzsimmons

Sean Fitzsimons

recalled by Andy Fitzsimons

Sean was born in 1930, the youngest of three boys, in inner city Dublin. After attending a local school, he left at the age of 14 and got his first job in the post room of a Dublin accountancy firm. He later left this position, and started work for Gill & Co. a church furnishing company, later to become Gill & McMillan publishers. After a year or two working in their O'Connell St. shop and learning the ropes, he became a sales rep for the company, travelling all over Ireland and the UK for the next 25 years supplying Churches, Convents and Monastic Orders with religious furnishings and church fittings.

As a teenager and young man, he was a very keen cyclist, and a member of "Lorraine Cycling Club" where he won a number of trophies, and held the record for distance Tandem Cycling until the day he died. Most weekends, he and a bunch of his pals would go off cycling around Ireland. He would think nothing of catching the ferry to Liverpool, then cycling to Coventry (about 120 miles) to visit his brother Paddy. One summer holiday, he even cycled to Rome and back. (This may be slightly exaggerated; Trains and Ferries played a part)

During the late 1950's Sean "discovered" the Shannon, and was a participant of the first Shannon Boat Rally on a boat called "Tia Maria"

III He had such a great time on this Rally that he returned the following year when he hired an old Guinness barge, the "St. Mary", from the Hotel in Lanesborough.

In those days, most of the boats on the Rally were small lake craft, 2 or 4 berths, and so a converted Barge automatically became the "Party Boat". Sean subsequently bought the barge, and renamed her "Ye Iron Lung". He was now completely hooked.

While still working as a salesman for Gills, he would travel Ireland working during the week, but would spend most weekends in Athlone or up and down the Shannon. In 1970 he bought a bar in Athlone, from Sean O'Brien, named Sean's Bar. This not only became known as a great "River Pub" but also became famous for its Traditional music and Folk sessions. Today, it can be found in the Guinness Book of Records as the oldest pub in the British Isles.

Sean served as Treasurer of Athlone Branch for approximately 30 years, and he was largely responsible for building and maintaining membership numbers, and a healthy bank balance, which contributed to branch activities such as providing mooring buoys & jetties at Athlone town, Ballykeeran, Portrunny, and Lecarrow.

He organised the reprint, sale and distribution of Harry Rice's book *Thanks for the Memory* in both 1974, which built a healthy Development fund for the various branch projects and also for the ben-

Sean's boat, "Ye Iron Lung"

efit of various other organisations such as Athlone Sub-Aqua club, Athlone Boat Club, RCAG, etc. and again in 2002, which is currently benefiting the Dunrovin Trust redevelopment fund, and reprints of old charts (1808) of Lough Ree & Lough Derg, which were found in Dunrovin and also benefit the fund.

Sean also organised the reprint of the book *Green and Silver*, which raised over £10,000 for the Royal Canal Amenity Group.

In 2001 Sean sold "The Lung" to his nephew as it became more difficult to get crew, and bought a cruiser "An Spailpin Eile" so he was still able to spend time on the river. Unfortunately, in 2003, following what started as a minor injury, Sean lost his leg and became wheelchair bound. But, despite his handicap, continued to enjoy the waterways, entering Rallies and enjoying the 'Craic'.

From 1960 until his death in 2011, Sean supported Rallies and events all over the country. He became totally involved in the preservation and improvement of the Shannon, the Royal Canal, the Shannon-Erne Waterway and all the inland waterways of Ireland. Today, those of us who benefit from all the work done by Sean and his peers over the years owe them a great debt of gratitude.

Rosemary Furlong

by Michael Martin

The name of Rosemary Furlong has been synonymous with the waterways of Ireland for over sixty years. Born in Athlone on 17th of September 1922 to Dr. T.P. Chapman and Dr. Gertrude Chapman, nee Rice, Rosemary spent all of her early years with her grandparents Dr T.W. Rice and Mrs Harriet Jane Rice in Portarlington Co Laois. They were parents of Col. Harry Rice, founder of The Inland Waterways Association of Ireland.

At eighteen years of age she returned to Athlone where she took up a position as assistant photographer with *The Westmeath Independent* Newspaper. Her keen interest in photography was to have huge historical significance in later years. Her many photos and cine movies which she recorded during the early Waterways Rallies have been used in several printed publications dealing with the Shannon and its lakes, including the DVD, *50 Years of Silver River* by Marc Gleeson.

One of Rosemary's many tasks during the early Rallies was the organisation of "The Harry Rice Essay Competition". The cup itself was one of Harry's racing trophies which he had won while serving in India and was awarded annually to the younger Ralliests for the best essay describing a boating trip on the Shannon. Runners-up received book tokens. Rosemary saw to it that all entries received a prize of some sort.

She studied and graduated at Trinity Collage Dublin in the mid 1940s, following which she spent four years working in the Administrations Office of Trinity Collage as secretary to the senior tutor. In 1951 Rosemary married Dr. Norman Furlong in Dublin. In 1952 Norman joined the practice of Dr. Thomas P. Chapman at St. Pauls, Garden Vale, Athlone. They resided on the premises for many years before moving to their new bungalow at "Mallard" Coosan Point, Athlone. "Mallard" is situated next door to "Dunrovin" where Rosemary's uncle, Harry Rice resided with his wife Cynthia.

During their years at St. Pauls, Rosemary became deeply involved in the R.N.L.I. annual fundraising collection. St. Pauls was the nerve center for the yearly weekend drive. The collectors, led by Cynthia Rice, donned the garb of the Life Boat people, complete with yellow oilskins and sou'westers and blitzed the pubs of Athlone on the Saturday night. They made the proverbial killing.

To this day, Rosemary is a member and supporter of the R.N.L.I. Her commitment to the Lifeboats was acknowledged at the opening of the new station at Coosan Point in July 2013.

One of the most recognisable and loved boats on the inland waterways is the converted lifeboat "Francesca" owned and sailed by Norman and Rosemary for over forty-two years. They participated in all of the Shannon Rallies up to the time of Norman's failing health. They were equally skilled as helms people.

In the early 1960s, the Barrow Navigation had been the cause of some anxiety as through lack of use there was the danger that the waterway would fall into disrepair. To stimulate interest, the Carlow Branch of the I.W.A.I. called for a "cruise in company" from the Shannon to Carlow at Easter 1962. Six cruisers answered the call, three from Athlone, two from Dublin and one from Waterford. Of the three cruisers from Athlone, "Francesca" with Rosemary ,Norman and their six year old son Alan were on board. They completed the journey to Carlow with Mick Mannion on "Susan M" and Paddy Flynn on "Barracuda".

Rosemary and Norman spent many happy years at

their lake-side beloved "Mallard" until May 2007 when Norman finally lost his battle against a pulmonary illness which he fought courageously for ten years.

Rosemary Furlong ready with her camera

Their hospitality to visiting boats and crews to the harbour at "Mallard" was legendary among the mariners of the Inland Waterways. A keen gardener, an excellent cook and an avid reader,

Rosemary Furlong is a remarkable lady and life member of Athlone I.W.A.I.

David Killeen

recalled by Donal O'Siochain

David Killeen was a young man when he entered his first Shannon Rally, which I believe was Rally number two in 1962. However he was only a stripling when he first encountered the Shannon, as his family lived for years on the Barge "Gillaroo" at first in the Ardnacrusha tailrace where his father was one of the engineers in charge of building the dam, and after in Killaloe. As a schoolboy he showed early talent for farming as he fed his own

David Killeen in full sail

hens on the barge – the only swimming hens in Ireland!

Coming back to the 1962 Rally David distinguished himself by sailing without the benefit of an outboard all the way from Athlone to Carrick. This involved heaving the boat over at every bridge so they could pass under! This started a lifelong love of the river, and indeed the Rallies where his sailing cruiser "Gillaroo" is known throughout our waterways, and when he won the Premier Award in the early 80's David was able to announce he had spent twenty years becoming an overnight success. On that Rally he was accompanied by all his family – Eleanor his beloved wife and his children Maeve, Alice, Aisling and David Junior. All share his love of the river.

David was a founder member of the Slaney Branch of the Inland Waterways Association of Ireland and indeed is Life President of the Branch. He was instrumental in the branch's many cruises (I nearly said escapades) on the many canals and minor rivers in the Wexford area, not forgetting many Branch Rallies both on the Slaney and the Barrow rivers. Mainly because of David's sociability many members of the Association from faraway waterways including the Corrib and Erne have enjoyed the hospitality of the Slaney Branch on Rallies. In particular I will never forget the late and very much missed Christy Deacy washing Kay's hair every morning of a Rally to be repaid by Kay steering the boat as Christy dozed in the afternoon sun on the Slaney.

Apart from his Branch David had a great interest in Association affairs and was until recently a very long-standing member of the Council where his wisdom was of great benefit for many years. David lives for the Association and our waterways. Until recently he could be found literally paddling his canoe not only in Wexford but also on adventures like the Liffey descent. I can only gasp at his energy – and I can give him a fair few years!

It is not only our own waterways that David explores. Every year for the past eight years, David and Eleanor have visited Mike and Rosaleen Miller on their adventures in Europe. Over the years they have seen much of the French Canals, the Belgian Canals including the fantastic Boat Lift at Strepy-Thieu, some of the Dutch waterways and even the Kiel Canal in Germany.

In concluding may I wish David and Eleanor many more years of cruising with their friends both at home and abroad.

Syd Shine

recalled by Damien Delaney

Ask any of the older generation of boater from around the Athlone area how they got interested in boating and eight out of ten will tell you that Syd Shine introduced them to the waterways either as crew member on the "Fox" or on the Shannon One Design (SOD) sailing boat, or indeed on one of his many other boats.

Syd Shine and "Fox" have played an important role for the rivers and canals of Ireland – for their development and restoration, for cruising and sailing, for training and boatmanship, and for entertainment since the foundation of the IWAI, we hope that these few paragraphs will give you an insight into the life and activity of someone who has lived in harmony with the Waterways of Ireland for over ninety years.

Syd Shine's father was a builder by trade, but he also had a small farm near Clonmacnoise. Syd grew up there and learned his boating skills at an early age, rowing from Clonmacnoise and Clonown to Athlone with farm produce and turf for sale. Syd also bought, repaired, and sold boats, and in the process he "traded up" his fleet from an 18ft boat to a 36ft sailing boat called "Elfin", which he and his friends used to cruise all over the Shannon. He made his first trips to Dublin in 1934 along both the Grand Canal and the Royal Canal, bringing boats from Athlone for fitting out in Dublin.

Syd Shine (left) chatting to Reggie Goodbody

Syd attended the inaugural meeting of the Inland Waterways Association of Ireland in the Shelbourne Hotel in Dublin, at which the IWAI was formed in 1954, and he proudly displayed the photograph to prove that he was a founder member.

Also in 1954, Syd's father had built the Crescent Ballroom in Athlone, and it is here that the meeting to form the first Branch of the newly formed Inland Waterways Association of Ireland, the Athlone Branch, was held. Syd was one of the founder members of the Athlone Branch, and he also was a member of the first Council of the IWAI, and has remained a loyal, lifelong member and presently holds Honorary Life Member status.

As a young man, Syd's skill and love of boats and the waterways was recognised by Denis Madigan,

Chang-Sha, now owned and skippered by Colin Becker, is the oldest known boat on the waterway system

who operated the OPW maintenance barge "Fox". Denis asked Syd to promise to look after "Fox" when he (Denis) passed on. The "Fox" was decommissioned in 1956, and was stripped and lay derelict in the old canal in Limerick. It became a hazard and was about to be sunk or scrapped when Denis wrote to Syd regarding his promise to look after the "Fox". Syd already owned "Chang-Sha" at that time, and didn't really need another sixty foot boat, but he put in a sealed bid of £30, and then heard that someone else was bidding £40, so Syd upped his bid to £50 — and became the new owner of the "Fox". Following some fitting out and refurbishment Syd decided to live aboard the "Fox". Being a competent musician he brought and installed his Hammond Organ, and moored the "Fox" at the Watergate in Athlone, until 1999 when sadly, failing health required him to move to an adjacent nursing home.

Those of us who, 60 years later, can enjoy the pleasures of cruising the waterways of Ireland owe much to the founder members, who had the vision and the courage to take on the authorities in order that the right of navigation on the Shannon, and more recently on the canals would be secured for future generations. One of the "vehicles" to support their cause was the boat rally from Athlone to Carrick-on-Shannon, which they ran each year from 1954, and which developed in 1961 into what we now know as the Shannon Boat Rally. Syd was a prominent supporter and committee member of the Athlone Branch and of the Shannon Boat Rally in those early years, winning the Premier Award in 1963 and 1965 in his beloved "Fox", he served as Shannon Rally Commodore in 1989.

He has been involved for most of his life with the IWAI, at all Athlone Branch events. He was, until recently, a regular supporter of the Shannon Harbour Rally, the Corrib Rally, and the Erne Rally, and would still be supporting the Shannon rallies except that they clashed with his favourite events – the sailing regattas on Lough Ree and Lough Derg. Sailing at Lough Ree Yacht Club was his favourite pursuit where he was one of the more successful Shannon One Design sailors. He organised and almost single handed ran the Lough Ree Yacht Club through the lean times in the 50's, and was instrumental in sustaining activity at the club, which ultimately resulted in the wonderful facilities members enjoy today. He built and operated the Jolly Mariner Marina in the 70's, and donated the space for the Harry Rice Slipway on the site and brought the first floating filling station to the inland waterways of Ireland.

He ran the "Fox" almost as a training-ship; many of the students are now well-known names on the Shannon. He was a regular Shannon One-Design sailor who has been awarded Honorary Life Membership of both the Lough Ree and the Lough Derg Yacht Clubs. The trips to rallies and regattas, particularly the trip from Lough Ree to Lough Derg Yacht Club for the annual regatta, with the "Fox" swarming with young participants has been likened to an adventure of Huckleberry Finn – and truly they were. The sight of the "Fox" appearing around Urra Point and moving into Dromineer harbour with up to ten SODs in tow astern was always an emotional time and a signal that the regatta had begun.

He participated in an expedition with Athlone Branch IWAI, from Leitrim to the first lock on the Ballinamore-Ballyconnell canal back in the 1970s, long before its restoration. He has accumulated an invaluable archive of documents, photographs and mementoes of the "Fox", of his own activities and of the history of the waterways, and he has been a regular contributor to TV, Radio, and Newspaper media on the history of the Waterways.

The Saints — Athlone
Phone: Manager, Pat Noone, Claremorris 168

Syd's other love is music, and he has been involved in music all his life, with his own very successful band *Syd and the Saints* during the show-band era. He ran dances in the Crescent Ballroom in Athlone, where many of us learned to jive, foxtrot & waltz, stepping on the corns of some unfortunate girl in the process! He gave freely of his musical talent to enhance the entertainment at rallies, regattas, cruises and functions. His contribution to these events over many years is immeasurable. Syd was a constant source of encouragement to all users and lovers of our waterways and he gave unselfishly of his time and experience to all who called on him.

Rory O Hanlon

recalled by Charles Dunn

Rory O Hanlon was I believe one of the founder members of IWAI, a keen sailor with a huge appetite for adventure. Rory worked as a gynaecologist in Dublin, and sailed also with Douglas (and Ruth) Heard, who later bought the "Harklow" to venture on inland waterways. Rory sailed a Dragon class sailboat (the type still in use in Dun Laoghaire) "Firedrake" which had no engine, making cruising difficult. It also had only a "cuddy" rather than an enclosed cabin, which made cruising even more difficult. Rory brought his Dragon – with a Seagull outboard strapped on – up the river Shannon to assist the IWAI campaigners, insisting on "full airdraft" and requiring bridges to be opened for them as they made their way upstream on the river. I believe they came unstuck at the Lough Tap Railway Bridge, which did in fact open for them, but the signal and telephone cables overhead could not be removed to allow Rory proceed upstream. When the CIE boats were introduced this guaranteed a certain free airdraft all the way on the Shannon Navigation.

Rory later sailed his steel hulled gaff rigged yacht "Meermin" (owned by the King of Norway, but foundered and later recovered from the ocean depths off Cork) to Iceland and north to Spitzbergen.

Noel Murphy

recalled by Charles Dunn

I was only a young boy when my uncle Noel came to tell us of the "Dinghy Scramble" which he was arranging on Dublin's Grand Canal at Portobello, to promote use and renovation of the canal. The idea was to race your dinghy along the canal – using oars or outboard engine – from point to point. But you did have to port across the locks (most locks didn't work anyway at that time) and thus carrying an engine would slow you down. Noel

Celtic Canal Cruisers

approached us to see if we could entice the yachting community to bring their dinghies from Dun Laoghaire to bring up the numbers. I believe that the Dinghy Scramble ended due to difficulties obtaining insurance.

Noel was secretary or maybe even president of Dublin IWAI for a while, and an old film shows him working on the renovation of the Naas line.

Noel approached my father in the 1970s seeking premises to build lock gates. IWAI had by then decided to start renovating the canal themselves, and had cleared out locks in locations which were now ready to be fitted. There was hope that AnCO (later FAS) would provide labour to build the gates, and CIE had promised to crane the gates in once they arrived on site. Noel and IWAI were also seeking funding for timber. The ideal gate construction site would be in Dublin, near to their eventual installation site and also close to a ready labour force. But finding space – for free! – was a problem. I believe RCAG had a gate-making site somewhere along the Royal Canal, and I am not sure if IWAI eventually shared this.

As a child, my mother told me that her brother Noel had bought and renovated the two-storey house at the junction of the Kilbeggan Line with the Grand Canal. Being an architect, building renovation was his line, and being an IWAI member, he must have assumed that the Kilbeggan branch would one day re-open and his canalside cottage would become valuable. In later years I moored 67M alongside and chatted with the then owners, who recalled that they had bought it from a Dublin architect. Alas like Heather Thomas who spent 20 years building up Celtic Canal Cruisers, the nearby Kilbeggan line is as dry today as it was in the 1960s. Heather Thomas and Noel Murphy must indeed look down in wonder at what more the IWAI could achieve.

The River Barrow

Professor Joseph Johnston
recalled by Siobhan Kinahan (Great-granddaughter

August 2 1890 – 1972, Member of inaugural committee IWAI 1954

Joseph (Joe) Johnston was born the second youngest of seven siblings in Tomagh near Castle Caulfield, Co Tyrone. Both his parents were schoolteachers and they also had a family farm. Joe attended Trinity College Dublin where he attained a degree in Classics and Ancient History and went on to Oxford to obtain a second degree, returning to Trinity in 1913 to successfully complete a Fellowship. He married in 1914 and then started his Albert Khan Travelling Fellowship trip, which involved the newlyweds travelling to India, America, Java, Japan and China at a time of great turmoil with the outbreak of World War One. As a result of this trip Joe became more focused on economics, and back in Ireland developed interests in agriculture and the Co-operative movement. They had two children Maureen (1916-2002) and Roy (b 1929).

In the 1950s Professor Johnston was Chair of Applied Economics at Trinity College, a role specially created for him in recognition of his work in putting his economic theories into practice particularly in relation to agriculture. He was also serving his fourth and final term as a member of Seanad Eireann, having been elected three times in the University of Dublin Constituency and nominated by the Taoiseach, de Valera in 1951.

It is the record of contributions to the Seanad that demonstrate his interest in the preservation of the inland waterways of Ireland. In particular his speech as part of the debate of the Appropriation Bill in November of 1953 Joe draws attention to the book *Green and Silver* and commented of the author, L T C Rolt: "He might only be the pioneer of hundreds like him if only we developed this magnificent highway instead of strangling it by building a fixed bridge at Athlone." At the time it was felt that the modernization of Ireland should focus on roads as the new form of transport and the inland waterways were outdated and slow. So to suggest that the waterways were a potential tourist attraction and should therefore influence how roads were constructed was quite radical.

Joe finishes addressing the Seanad by saying "It should be a part of our national policy to develop all our waterways to the greatest possible extent." It is not surprising to find Prof J Johnston, just two months after this contribution in the Seanad, listed as one of the elected officers at the inaugural meeting of the Inland Waterways Association of Ireland as he so clearly identified with the aims and objectives of the IWAI to maintain, protect and restore the inland waterways.

Around this time Joe and his family lived at Grattan Lodge in Vicarstown, which is on the Barrow line of the Grand Canal, and so had great opportunity to witness at first hand the condition of the canals at the time and their lack of use. Overall Joe's interest in the waterways was primarily in the way they intersected with his main work as an economist, but as such he viewed them as a valuable and underutilised asset to Ireland.

Tom Maher

Tom Maher jnr

The Maher family (formerly from the Bush Hotel, Carrick-on-Shannon) has a long history of involvement with Carrick IWAI and boating on the North Shannon generally.

Tom J Maher (1937-2012) was well known for his passionate support of boating on the North Shannon and was a keen supporter of IWAI, having been secretary and Chairman of the Carrick branch for many years. Tom was also instrumental in bringing boat hire business to Carrick along with many other initiatives that made Carrick into a great boating destination.

Tom acquired his love affair of the river from his father Tom F Maher (TF Maher) who was a

Tipperary man who married into the McDermott family, owners of the Bush Hotel. TF Maher had a motor boat on the Shannon from the 1950s called "Naomh Ronan" and in September 1962 was one of the founding members of the "revived" Carrick branch of IWAI – formed by the merger of the Carrick-on-Shannon Yacht Club and the, by then, dormant Carrick IWAI branch. TF Maher was appointed Chairman and Secretary of the Branch at that meeting which took place in the Bush Hotel, and so commenced the important role of the Bush and the Maher family in IWAI life.

TF Maher was one of the men responsible for establishing the Shannon Boat Rally and regularly entered his boat "Naomh Ronan" in the Rallies until his death in 1966. In the mid 1960's, Tom J Maher bought his own boat, "Bushbaby", which received great use over the next 30 years. "Bushbaby" would often be seen on the North Shannon trailing a menagerie of other vessels from Tom's speedboat to a sailing dingy, canoe and windsurfer all tied together by some recycled rope! As a result, he became affectionately known to friends on the river as the "Dromod Mariner" (a reference to the junk shop man in Dromod)!

After TF Maher's death in 1966, Tom J Maher continued the family's proud tradition within IWAI and became commodore of the 1969 Shannon Boat Rally that started in Carrick that year. The programme for the event refers to the opening night being in "The Bush Hotel (followed by a Hooley)". The focus of those early Rallies was

Grand Canal barges at Dromineer

rightly always on having fun and promoting camaraderie. Tom maintained an active involvement in IWAI for the rest of his life, quietly dedicating significant time and energy for over fifteen years to a cause very close to his heart: the re-opening of the Ballinamore – Ballyconnell Canal. It gave Tom enormous pride and pleasure to witness that project come to fruition in the 1990s and to see first-hand the benefits of cross-border cooperation.

Dad was commodore of the Rally in 1969. Mum recalls helping out with the first night Rally event with their first child Conor – exactly a month old that night – in her arms. This was the start of the next generation of Mahers' life on the Shannon. Mum recalled a funny anecdote from that Rally for me this week. Dad, Mum and 4-week-old Conor were on "Bushbaby" for the Rally. Mum duly "babysat" her new born each evening on "Bushbaby" as Dad mingled with other boaters – as he did! On one night, Dad offered Mum a night off and said he and Bill Child would baby-sit Conor and that Mum should go onboard the "Ye Iron Lung" for their party. Not wanting to miss the legendary Lung party, Dad and Bill took a two way radio, strapped the button in the Transmit position, placed it in the carry cot onboard "Bushbaby" beside sleeping Conor, kept the other radio with them and toddled off to the Lung, much to my mother's surprise! Their ingenuity ensured they didn't miss the Lung party, Conor was safe (apparently!), slept soundly and a good night was had by all – typical of the fun we all had on the Rally over the years.

Since Tom's sudden passing in January 2012, his family (wife Rosaleen, children Conor, Ronan, Tom D and Claire) have been contacted by many "river people" to say how Tom inspired them to get into boating. Perhaps the best way to explain this ambassador type role that Tom played for over 50 years is to quote Paul Garland, the then IWAI President, from the obituary he wrote for Tom in 2012:

"The first time I came on the Shannon and I met Tom Maher I thought it was a unique privilege as he came alongside in his smart little speedboat and offered to take us out for a spin on the river. Later he invited us to come up to the Bush Hotel for complementary showers. What is surprising is that day in the early sixties was just a typical day

for Tom. Many people have shared this privilege, and many have taken to the river because of Tom. This was the nature of his generosity and his enthusiasm for all things river related and life in general."

Eric Timon "The Pooka Man"

recalled by Helen Timon

Eric Timon with Amow

Eric was born on 16th March 1919 on the shores of the river Shannon in Athlone Co Westmeath. He spent his early years fishing on Lough Ree in a lake boat. His young life on the river was cut short by World War II and he eloped to Belfast to marry the love of his life. Many years passed before he could return to his beloved Shannon but even then life was cruel, and work sent him to Dublin and Howth where he settled by the sea. He had heard of the IWAI and the rallies they were holding and he set about to build his own boat to join. In 1963 Eric received his boat pack to build his own boat. This was the start of "Amow" (All My Own Work or when he was asked what it meant he told them it was the name of St Patrick's cat!). She was complete for the 1965 rally, she was a little sea boat, 16ft long with

Eric enjoying a pint

a 20hp Johnson. Many people will remember it chained to a lamp post on the way up the hill in Howth. "Amow" served his needs well but he decided he needed something bigger so "Amow II" was started. She was a 50ft Ferro cement wide beam boat. A labour of love which he scuttled in Balscadden Bay where they say the best Lobsters are caught (Another story)! Many boats later he bought "Amow III", New Year's Eve in Kilgarvan with a force nine blizzard blowing, what a journey! At this stage the Derg Rally had started and Eric was doing the Shannon and Derg Rallies back to back. He was winning the Talent competitions each year with his Dittys and hence the Ditty Competition was started, it took the pressure off him and kept the Pookas at bay. Eric will be remembered for his early morning swims on all rallies. He produced two books which were a compilation of stories and ditties over the years. His love of the inland waterways wasn't confined to Shannon and he travelled the canals also despite the little people turning the canal around on him one night! His love of the Shannon was instilled into his family members and today his daughter Helen continues the family tradition on "Amow V". His love of messing about on boats lives on in his son Eric who still messes around on a different kind of boat, Lt Cmdr. in the Navy!

John Weaving

recalled by Brian Cassells

John Weaving with his forever friend on board his barge "The Peter Farrell"

I first met John Weaving at Leitrim on his canal boat the "Peter Farrell", he was there as part of a work party in the days when our organisation was lobbying for the re-opening of the Ballinamore/Ballyconnell canal. I had driven down from Enniskillen with the late Alan Giff and never having been to such work parties before, I certainly did not know what to expect. I recall John as a tall slim man; with a quiet reserved personality certainly not interested in his attire but obviously highly respected by those around him. This wasn't his neck of the woods; indeed I wondered just where he was from and where exactly he lived. Tentatively I asked questions of those who acknowledged the new boy and what unfolded enlightened me to an amazing acquaintance, which for me was all too brief. Here was a man who believed passionately in the potential of what this restored waterway could achieve, this was a knowledgeable well-read person, a bachelor through and through who was at peace with the world.

John's base was the Lecarrow canal off Lough Ree, an area he knew intimately, on board with him that day were others who I subsequently got to know as heroes of the river, Syd Shine, one I had encountered in younger days on stage with his band at a dance in Armagh, and Sean Fitsimmons of Sean's bar in Athlone fame, often referred to as the oldest pub in Ireland! All three were younger versions of friends I became acquainted with in later life, men who were inspirational visionaries of the waterways. Where John went the two dogs went, they were ever by his side, I recall meeting all three years later in a lake boat heading for Athlone acknowledged by his friendly wave. The canal boat, an original horse-drawn B boat had everything on board, a perpetual storehouse of posts, fenders, engines and bits of engines, instruments and of course tools and tools and tools.

Meeting John Weaving was an enrichment, a memorable and unforgettable experience that I genuinely feel the better for, a quiet man, highly regarded by all who knew him, perhaps he shunned much of modern culture but I know he found contentment in his simple way of life, a man loved by his pets and at peace with the world; is there a lesson here for us craving for the next gadget, I like to think so.

Eddie Slane

recalled by Brian Cassells

Eddie Slane

Few people over the years have devoted more time and energy into restoring the Royal Canal than Eddie Slane. Eddie was in from the start of the Royal Canal Amenity Group (RCAG); sadly he never did see the realisation of his dream, the re-opening of the complete canal as he passed away in 1999. Eddie served as Honorary Secretary and as Chairman of the group until his untimely death and without doubt was its champion fundraiser. Eddie was a 'hands on' guy; he was happiest organising work parties and in the early days of the group was often to be found on the outskirts of Dublin at Castleknock and Ashtown. Shortly after his death a seat was erected at Moran's Bridge outside Mullingar, a lasting testament to a 'Royal' stalwart.

Typical of Eddie's commitment was hiring the National Concert Hall in Dublin and organising a show to raise funds for the project, many of his colleagues were sceptical of the plan but with enthusiasm and gusto, the show was a sell out, indeed this was one of many similar fund raising events. When an event was organised in a neighbouring area Eddie travelled to attend in his small cruiser, always making the statement at least that section was open for business.

Jim McGarry

recalled by Brian Cassells

Jim & George McGarry

Jim McGarry was Mr Lough Neagh, a man who lived by the Lough, who worked on the Lough and who created boats suited for the Lough. The McGarry family had long been associated with Ardmore Boatyard situated near Glenavy on the eastern shoreline quite close to Belfast International Airport. His father was a respected boat builder, a man who built real boats, where the timbers were steamed and bent and copper fastened to the ribs, boats that were built to last, some indeed still giving proud service over half a century later.

I first met Jim skippering the "Maid of Antrim" on evening nautical manoeuvres on Lough Neagh; we'd left from Antrim, a sort of office party out for an evening sail. I was drawn to him instantly, his warm endearing jovial personality was refreshing, I found myself straight away relaxing in this man's company, and he had time to talk yet ever watchful as he piloted the boat through the dark waters. Jim knew every mood of the Lough, while the Maid was equipped with modern navigational aids you felt they were there as a check for his vast knowledge. He with his brother George had bought the boat on the Clyde and were operating her as a pleasure boat on Lough Neagh, it was very much a family business supplemented by the boat building enterprise his father had established years before.

The McGarry family came to prominence during World War Two when they worked in support of the airborne forces, British, American and Canadian who used both Lough Neagh and Lough Erne as bases and for practicing manoeuvres. These practically minded men retrieved crashed aircraft, located buoys, and laid bombing targets, in fact anything that was asked of them. Jim told the lovely story of cycling along the shore road trying to keep pace with the open cockpitted aircraft flying along the shoreline and waving to the pilot and gunner. Once he proudly showed me the canvas diving suit, complete with copper bell top and lead weighted boots in one of the sheds stored yet never again to be used.

At heart Jim was a family man obvious by the love he had for his wife and children and they for him; but he was a fisherman, a boat designer and a boat builder. He designed and constructed fishing boats, day boats and motor sailors, his knowledge and skill were vast, he was well read and knowledgeable, he wrote a number of articles for our magazine which displayed a hidden talent, he was a popular speaker at Historical Society lectures, sadly he was taken from us too early; he is missed by his family first but also the gap in the Lough Neagh community could never be filled.

resource as a mecca for tourists. Apart from the boat hire business which he established virtually single handed, he designed numerous yachts and sailing dinghies. Ireland has produced more than its fair share of great leisure boat designers, Donie Conlan of Carnadoe Marina speaks eloquently of this man, and indeed Donie was trusted with bringing many of his plans to fruition.

George O'Brien Kennedy

recalled by Brian Cassells

George O'Brien Kennedy was born in 1912, and in his book *Not all at Sea* he states "Man was beginning to take to the air" when he was born. I'm not sure if he ever was a member of the Association but as a naval designer he designed many of the first hire boats ever to grace the Shannon. For a number of years he worked in shipyards in England and achieved international recognition as a naval architect during World War Two eventually moving to India where he designed harbour tugs, launches as well as many other associated vessels. In 1960 he returned to the Shannon quickly recognising the potential of this amazing

Christy Deacy

recalled by Michael J Hynes

Any history of the Corrib Branch would be incomplete if it did not acknowledge the contributions of Christy Deacy. His enormous contribution to both the Corrib Branch and the National Organisation deserves to be recognised. He had a passion for the Corrib, boating and sailing and all of his boats were sailing boats. There are many stories about his first boat, a small sailing dinghy called "The Pelican", in which he and his new wife Kay sailed and camped, much to the dismay of Christy's father who feared for another man's daughter being drowned by his son's escapades. This was followed by a home-built Glen 17 which was followed by a modified version of the Maurice

Griffith's designed Eventide 26. Later came "Miss Claire", a massive steel hulled sailing boat of 36 feet with a lifting keel, named after his daughter Claire. The hull was constructed in Borth in Wales and was completed by Christy in his workshop in Renmore.

Christy played a key role in the construction of much of the infrastructure now enjoyed by members of the IWAI who cruise the Corrib. What would life be like in the absence of the piers on Inchagoill and at Maam Bridge? A plaque honouring his contribution was unveiled at the Maam pier; it reads:

"Inland Waters Association of Ireland Lough Corrib Branch Dedicates this Plaque to the Memory of Christy Deacy 1947 – 2003".

Without Christy's initiative, enthusiasm, knowledge and skills, it is doubtful if these projects would have been brought to fruition. While others talked and discussed, Christy just went ahead and did it. During his Presidency of Corrib Rowing and Yachting Club in Galway (1980-82) he oversaw the construction of the boatshed which is routinely used by members of the IWAI Corrib Branch for painting and repairs.

Christy was a man of incredible energy, knowledge and experience. His engineering skills were legendary and I doubt if there is an IWAI member of his reign who did not benefit from these at one time or another. His forte was in coming up with

Christy in working garb

simple solutions to intractable problems, a skill that also served him well in his professional life. While he did not suffer fools gladly and was known to robustly admonish people who made silly mistakes, he never refused assistance and was always at hand to assist boats in distress. He was extremely generous with his time. Since moving to his residence in Lisloughrey, he had many a callout to assist boats that had broken down, had gone aground or had other issues.

Christy was also very much involved in the National scene and was a Council member for many years. He rarely missed a Council meeting irrespective of where they were held. Once having travelled to a meeting in Mullingar in very frosty weather, he was not pleased to find an apology from the Athlone contingent stating they were unable to travel due to the poor condition of the roads. He and Kay were regular attendees at the Shannon, Erne and Slaney rallies.

Christy was a very generous man and he and Kay hosted visitors from the other branches on "Miss Claire". At rallies "Miss Claire" was like a drive-through restaurant such was the hospitality. He was particularly generous to visitors who often came with small boats that had very limited cooking facilities. If he had a weakness, it was his inability to appreciate the alcohol content of spirits. He was a virtuoso in the art of the "Pioneer's pour".

Christy's untimely passing in August 2003 came as a great shock to those of us who knew him and appreciated his contributions to our enjoyment of the Corrib. When we old-timers visit each other's boats during weekends on the Corrib, it is rare to go home without a mention of Christy Deacy at some point in the evening. It is a measure of his stature that we still remember him with such affection some ten years after his passing.

Ní bheidh a leithide ann arís.

Alan Giff

recalled by Brian Cassells

November 2010 saw the sad passing of one of the great Lough Erne characters, the big smiling man who was larger than life and who lived fully his waterway dream. Alan Giff kept the IWAI flame alive in Northern Ireland for many years being Chair of the original Lough Erne Branch, renaming it the Northern Ireland Branch when the Scarva Branch ceased to operate; this enabled a watchful eye to be kept on the other abandoned navigations. Alan

Alan Giff

fully participated in many waterway activities; he was an active supporter of the Lough Erne Rally and was a past Commodore. Alan enjoyed a varied career, as a highly respected journalist, horticulturist and latterly running the 'Moorings' restaurant, marina and boat repair business at Bellnaleck.

Alan was a colourful character who had a huge influence on waterway developments in the North, he laboured tirelessly for the re-opening of the Shannon Erne Link and was an avid supporter of the campaign to re-open the Ulster Canal. The waterway family was the poorer having lost someone who was indefatigable and larger than life itself.

Paddy Hatton

recalled by Brian Cassells

I've met some amazing people through my travels associated with IWAI but few left an indelible impression like the late Paddy Hatton; Paddy was a sincere Christian gentleman, someone you quickly realised was different, generous with his time and

Paddy Hatton

knowledge and friendship. He was a true Wexford and Slaney enthusiast, someone who knew the river intimately, his smile was infectious, and his humorous stories brought a smile to all in his company. Paddy was modest regarding his practical skills; I've heard the stories of how he built a canoe in his aunt's house and had to remove the window to get it out and to crown it all she agreed to give her daughter Mary's hand in marriage. Mary still misses Paddy, she told me so recently; not surprising really as he was such a special person; haven't we all asked the question, why does our Lord call the nicest people home first?

Reggie Redmond,

recalled by Brian Cassells

I first met Reggie over twenty years ago; it was my first visit to the Annual General Meeting of the Association and was held in the Royal Irish Automobile Association in Dawson Street in Dublin. I had heard his name mentioned many times in previous years in connection with motor racing, even from the legendary days of racing around the streets of Dunboyne. When Reggie realised there was a 'new boy' from the North

Reggie Redmond

he strode forward with that infectious smile and grasped my hand in welcome; what made this different was because it was so sincere and so genuine. In all the time I knew him he was a true loyal friend, one who could always be trusted.

This began a long association with one of life's gentlemen, a sincere Christian man who had high moral standards and a delightful warm personality. The loss of Sheila, Reggie's wife bore heavy on his mind; I recall him sitting in our living room telling me about her, tears were in his eyes as he fondly remembered their journey through life together. He was so proud of the children and grandchildren and what they had and were achieving in life.

Reggie was a meticulous treasurer of the Inland Waterways Association; he had a personal relationship with each branch treasurer and they were all totally supportive and viciously loyal to him. He formalised their reporting process, insisting that everyone completed his form which was to be forwarded to him with a copy of the bank statement, no fudges were ever tolerated. If a branch treasurer didn't return the form completed properly, they were named and shamed; the converse was also true; Reggie took great delight telling all assembled that such and such a branch were first in with their returns and that they were correct in every detail.

When it came to the AGM of the Association, Reggie presented the accounts and had copies for all present; it is fair to say he didn't particularly like being asked questions but when the accounts were put to the meeting all present stood and sang "For he's a jolly good fellow"; even though Reggie was a modest man, he thoroughly enjoyed the acclamation.

Reggie was an experienced boatman; he knew and loved Lough Ree intimately, he knew the quiet anchorages, the secluded bays, he often talked of Galey Bay, Curraghmurragh Bay and Barley Harbour; thankfully he was persuaded to put pen to paper and his article published in *Inland Waterway News* is still consulted and accepted as the definitive guide to Lough Ree.

L.T.C Rolt

recalled by Brian Cassells

LTC Rolt is seen as one of the father figures of our sister British organization, Inland Waterways Association, indeed he served as its first secretary. His publication of *Green and Silver* and the success of the IWA in Great Britain prompted the folk on this side of the Irish Sea to found the Association that would save our waterways. Lionel Thomas

Caswall Rolt, always known as Tom was a prolific writer with thirty-three books to his credit covering the waterways, railways and biographies of some great British engineers. His boat Cressy was a converted narrow boat in which he and his first wife Angela cruised the declining waterways of England. Green and Silver his account of the Irish waterways was first published in 1946, wartime in Ireland was known as "The Emergency" this was a time of petrol shortages and declining use of the waterways. After extensive written enquiries, Rolt located a twenty-six foot boat "Le Coq" supplied with a ten foot dingy which he could hire from a gentleman in Athlone called Mr John Beahan. The book basically describes a journey through rural Ireland from Battlebridge near Leitrim, on the upper reaches of the navigable Shannon to Lough Derg, travelling by both the Royal and Grand canals. Bunny and Betty Goodbody, founding members of IWAI, in their boat "Phoenix" were among the group who greeted the Rolts when they reached Lough Derg Yacht Club.

Tom Rolt out for a ride in the Sleive Bloom Mountains

Billy Beattie

recalled by Kildare Branch

Billy Beattie was a founding member of Kildare IWAI way back in 1984.

His love of the inland waterways saw him cruise the Shannon, the Barrow and the Canals for almost half a century where he became well known for his colorful personality and was christened "Billy Bee". Billy had many boats but his pride was "Sylvette", which he shared with Dr Maurice Davin-Power.

Excerpt from *Sylvette – the Shannon tour of 1977* by Maurice Davin-Power.

"All is not well. There is an air of dumb insubordination amongst the crew. Their work was done in a patchy manner with sullen faces. Muttering in corners was observed by one officer. The Captain and Mate, having urgent business to discuss, proceeded to the Athlunkard Bar. Here they were delayed by sundry matters and on their return at 23.50 hrs, the crew had abandoned ship! Desertion was feared, but they returned at 03.00 hrs again the worst for drink! Action was not taken, lest they be driven berserk, but it was noted in the log. All in all it was a night of fear." Next day at 11.00hrs "A hang-dog crew, conscious of their guilt, went about their work in a tolerable fashion". PK

Mick Clinton

recalled by Kildare Branch

Well, do you know something?

Any time you pulled into a harbour and saw "Blackthorn" moored up you were assured of an evening of music and craic at the hands of Mick and Fran.

Mick was also a skilled story teller and often he would stop his music in response to some conversation and put the banjo down on his lap, lean forward on it then chuckle and say "Well…do you know something …."

Sadly Mick Clinton passed away on the 1st September 2009. Mick's involvement with the Royal Canal Amenity Group followed a chance meeting with Chairman, Eddie Slane on the canal side at Kilcock. Their ensuing discussion centered on ways of staunching the leaking bank and of restoring water to the weed filled harbor. Eddie was so impressed that, without delay, Mick was invited to come and discuss his proposals with the RCAG committee at its next meeting.

The result was the formation of the Kilcock Branch of the RCAG, with Mick as Chairman; that was in June 1982. In no time at all, Mick's plans were put into action and in less than twelve months the whole harbour area and the fifteenth level were transformed. This proved to be the start of an eight year long programme of work carried out in collaboration with AnCO, and later with the OPW. With Mick at the helm, the team purchased two dragline excavators and extended the waterway from Leixlip to the Long Level. Mick derived enormous pleasure from the Irish waterways and in return his mechanical skills enabled him to make a huge contribution to the restoration of the Royal Canal.

As a tribute to Mick, Kildare IWAI inaugurated the Mick Clinton Perpetual Plaque – an award for outstanding contribution to the Branch.

Bob Sharpe
recalled by Kildare Branch

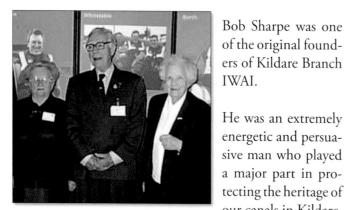
Bob Sharpe

Bob Sharpe was one of the original founders of Kildare Branch IWAI.

He was an extremely energetic and persuasive man who played a major part in protecting the heritage of our canals in Kildare. He was President of the IWAI and Chair

of Kildare IWAI; such was his hard work that he was made Honorary President of Kildare IWAI. In May 2001 at the Barbican Centre, London, the Duke of Kent presented Bob Sharpe with the prestigious RNLI Gold Medal Award. He was chairman of the Kildare Branch of the RNLI and up to the day of his passing, he was selling pins and raising money for this worthy cause.

Father PJ Murphy
recalled by Kildare Branch

Father PJ Murphy

Father PJ Murphy (1935-1975) encouraged people in the local community to put effort into restoring the old Robertstown Grand Hotel as a canal museum and community centre and organized a very successful series of annual period banquets and canal festivals.

Ruth Delany in *The Grand Canal of Ireland* states: "There was considerable focus on the canal at nearby Robertstown and in 1974 the old 19th lock on the Barrow Line was re-opened, making a convenient round trip for passengers on the Robertstown canal boat, up the Milltown feeder through the old

19th lock (Ballyteague) and back along the Barrow Line to Lowtown. The tragic death of the prime mover in all these activities, Father PJ Murphy, in a car accident on 8 November 1975, cast a great shadow over these efforts. 'Robertstown has lost a revered pastor and inspired community leader'.

The photographs from this era, some seen in our Waterways Gallery – Robertstown Canal Festas 1965-1975, give an indication of the success of these events.

Ruth Delany

by Brian Cassells and Padraic O Brolchain

Ruth Delany

I first met Ruth Delany nearly thirty years ago, this lady; small in stature has proved to me to be a loyal and supportive friend, generous with her vast knowledge and resources of the inland waterways and ever willing to gently give of her immense knowledge and comprehension of our waterway heritage. I recall her agreeing to give a lecture in Craigavon and when the late Brum Henderson, founder of Ulster Television and the Ulster Waterways Group heard of her intending visit, he readily agreed to chair the event, an occasion that is still vividly recalled some thirty years later. To say Ruth is acclaimed internationally is no over statement, indeed her contribution to the history of Ireland's waterways is immense, it virtually gives the complete picture. Ruth's books, from her *Shell Guide to the River Shannon* via her book *Ireland's Inland Waterways* to *The Shannon Navigation* tell the complete story of Ireland's waterways. Ruth was born in 1930, educated at Glengara Park School and Trinity College Dublin where she gained a Masters in economic history, lived for a period in Belfast and now resides with her daughter in Killiney. Ruth's first husband was Dr Vincent Delany and after his sad passing she married Douglas Heard who again shared Ruth's passion for the waterways. Ruth is of the old style, a lady in every sense of the word and generous with her time and knowledge, a truly lovely person.

Ruth Heard (Delany); A personal perspective by Padraic O Brolchain.

I first met Ruth on the Barrow when I was living in Carlow and was a member of the Barrow Branch. Carlow hosted a rally which was attended by several boats from Dublin. Douglas Heard was alive at the time and filming and their boat Harklow made the journey.

In 1973 I moved to Dublin and very soon after became enmeshed in the Dublin Branch of the Inland Waterways, first with Frank Blake as Chair and then becoming secretary with Peter Hanna. Our committee meetings were quite informal and at that time mainly held in different homes. Ruth was a very regular attendee. When we had work parties or any other outdoor event she was always there, helping and making a film record.

At the beginning I was slightly in awe of this person who had written and done so much for the Waterways, and who had been there from the very beginning. Her knowledge of the history of the system was impressive, but what struck one was her openness and friendliness, and her keen interest in everything to do with the waterways. She was willing to help in any way she could and could always be counted on if we needed a speaker, or a guide for a walk. Her annual film show was a very popular event. Another thankless task Ruth performed was the editing and publishing of the Newsletter, she wrote most of it also, as contributors were few and hard to motivate. Nothing has changed.

Alf Delany was president from 1967 to 1977; as a result the suggestion was then made that future Presidents should serve for a three-year term, Bill Child replaced Alf and Bill was followed by Ruth Delany. It was further agreed meetings should be held in Mullingar, thus all delegates had to travel and as a consequence there was an incentive to have shorter meetings. Much to Ruth's surprise but not to anyone else's, she was an excellent President and chaired the meetings with a gentle but very firm hand. Under her guidance the IWAI began a new phase of its existence and began to grow into the organisation it is today.

In later years I was one of a group, which included Ruth, on a trip to the 2005 World Canal conference in Sweden. On the way she said that it was the first time she had been to Sweden other than by sailing boat! This reminded us that the Inland waterways were not the only world inhabited by Ruth. Her second husband Douglas Heard was an intrepid ocean going yachtsman and his film archive is an invaluable record of early days at sea and of course the waterways.

It was a very good trip and Ruth proved to be good company. Her interest in all matters relating to canals and inland navigation made for many a pleasant conversation, more of interest however to the male members of the group. Ruth does not do small talk.

Ruth's first husband Vincent Delany was one of the founders of IWAI and it is as Ruth Delany that she first wrote and continues to use this as her nom de plume.

Dr. Ian Bath

Noel Spaine, Vice President RCAG

In the Ireland of many great voluntary figure heads, all working to promote their particular causes, the Inland Waterways Association of Ireland have been gifted with one such individual who has devoted many years in promoting the cause of Ireland's inland waterways. I refer of course to Dr Ian Bath.

Dr. Ian Bath

Ian's early introduction to our waterways goes back to the mid 1960's, when he occasionally walked the banks of the then derelict Royal Canal in the Castleknock area of County Dublin. But it was not until 1969 and having read Tom Rolt's book *Green and Silver* and the epic account of his journey through the Royal in 1946, that Ian's interest in the Royal was aroused. He began to explore the outer reaches of this waterway.

In 1973 Dr Ian attended a public meeting in Maynooth under the auspices of "An Taisce" to discuss the future of the Royal Canal. But this meeting was inconclusive. Joining the Dublin Branch of IWAI, Dr Ian wrote to the IWAI secretary expressing a wish to see formed a Royal Canal restoration society.

As a result of that letter Dr Ian was invited to a meeting of the Dublin Branch Committee, and after much discussion, a decision was taken to form a small sub-committee on which Ian was invited to sit. The Committee's first task was to take responsibility for mounting a display of maps and photographs at the forthcoming Dublin Boat Show.

Thus his campaign to save the Royal Canal had begun. In April 1974, with new found enthusiasm, Ian called a public meeting in Coolmine Community School, Blanchardstown, at which there was a unanimous decision to form a group based in this area which would soon be known as the Royal Canal Amenity Group.

Under Dr Ian's leadership, the RCAG set up voluntary work parties clearing overgrown tow paths and debris from lock gate chambers etc, while his IWAI sub-committee kept pressure on the powers that be to ensure that nothing would be done that would obstruct restoration of the Royal Canal.

From 1974 onwards, the RCAG, the IWAI sub-committee and the Athlone branch of IWAI worked in parallel. Dr Ian and his band of volunteers achieved remarkable success; from humble beginnings to major projects such as dredging the canal bed and restoring water levels, building a workshop at Confey, new slipways, the setting up of a lock gate manufacturing plant in Watling Street in Dublin together with numerous other ANCO programmes all requiring a high profile fundraising programme.

While all this voluntary work continued, Dr Ian still found time to spread his network westward, forming new RCAG branches within the many communities along the banks of the Canal. His ability to keep the cause of the restoration of the Royal in the public domain is shown strongly in his many media contributions to such publica-

A proud day for Dr. Ian Bath with the re-opening of the Royal Canal

behalf of myself and every member of IWAI, the RCAG, and the many other linked associations – "Thank you Dr Ian for a job well done; Wishing you continued success!

tions as IW News, Royal Canal newsletter and UK Magazines. In 1986, and with the transfer of the Canals from CIE to OPW, Dr Ian found himself working closely with this Government agency, and his dream gathered momentum.

The fruits of his vision shone brightest, when in October 2010 Ian took his seat amongst the dignitaries for the official re-opening of the Royal Canal "main line" at Richmond Harbour in the village of Cloondara, Co Longford.

Dr Ian received many awards during his leadership, including the coveted "Endeavour Cup" presented by IWAI and the title of Honorary Life President of the Royal Canal Amenity Group.

May I conclude, in this the 60th year of the Inland Waterways Association of Ireland, by saying on

Exiting Richmond Harbour, from the Royal Canal to the Shannon

The Royal Canal

Athlone Branch IWAI took a keen interest in the progress of the restoration of the Royal Canal from the start, and they supported the great work being done by Ian Bath and the RCAG by participating in the first rallies on the long level from Thomastown to Fern's Lock in the mid 1970s, and by getting down and dirty at various bank clearing & clean-up work parties in the 1980s.

From 1974 to 1981, Ian Bath and his committee in Dublin succeeded in preventing the Royal Canal between Croke Park and the Liffey from being filled in and built upon. They also generated a large body of support in the Dublin, Maynooth, Mullingar, Abbeyshrule, Ballinacargy, and Athlone areas as, by then, some visible action was badly needed to keep up the momentum that the RCAG had established. The plan was to build lock gates so that selected levels could be restored and watered. The IWAI proclaimed 1981 as "The year of the Royal" – primarily as a fundraising year. Guinness Ireland offered, free of charge, a store at Watling Street, Dublin, and an AnCO/RCAG Community Youth Training Project was inaugurated in February 1981 for the construction of lock gates. Funding was sought from the various local authorities in Dublin, Kildare,

and Meath, but any funding granted had to be matched by RCAG. Some match funding was available from Dublin Branch and the Bank of Ireland, but the principle benefactor at that time was Athlone Branch. Michael Martin, Chairman of Athlone IWAI branch, who had experience in fundraising for various charities, organised a major limited draw, with tickets @ £60 each for prizes of two Toyota Corolla cars, and nine cash prizes of £100 each. The draw was held at a function in the Rustic Inn, Abbeyshrule, and Michael Martin handed over a cheque for £7400 to Ian Bath for the RCAG. This may not sound like a large sum of money, but in 1981 you could buy 2 Toyota Corollas for £7400, this coupled with matching funds from the local authorities was sufficient to provide the materials for three pairs of lock gates, which got the project started. Other funding sources came on stream later to keep the project moving, albeit slowly. Athlone IWAI also ran functions and raffles to support the Abbeyshrule & the Keenagh/Foigha RCAG branches, which also had restoration work in hand.

Eddie Slane, then the Chairman of RCAG, presented an illustrated history of the restoration, entitled " The Royal Canal – A Remarkable Recovery" on the 6th March 1992 in the Jolly Mariner in Athlone, which demonstrated the progress to date and the need for more support. Interest in the Royal was revived, and in October 1992 the Athlone Branch IWAI organised a work party to help with the bank clearing between Mosstown harbour and the 41st lock, near Keenagh. Following a hard day's work and with throats as dry as the canal we retired to Pat Newman's pub in Keenagh where we enjoyed the hospitality of the Newman family, Michael Blaney, and the Hall family. The conversation explored how Athlone Branch IWAI could help with the restoration to best effect, the RCAG had a FAS scheme running which provided the labour force for their bank clearing programme, their main problem appeared to be insufficient funds to cover the cost of a foreman and the insurance cover for the scheme. The insurance premium at the time was costing almost £1000 per year so we formed the opinion that fundraising would be our most practical and beneficial form of help. Athlone Branch IWAI presented a cheque for £500, to Keenagh / Foigha Branch RCAG, and the FAS workers in Keenagh also presented £100, such was their enthusiasm about the project, at a function on the 19th March 1993 in Newman's pub. Later in 1993, Athlone Branch IWAI launched a reprint of the book Green and Silver which was a resounding success, thanks to Sean Fitzsimons salesmanship, and the profit ensured an ongoing annual income for the RCAG for many years.

By this time there were separate FAS Community Youth Training Projects running in Ballinacargy, Abbeyshrule, Ballymahon and Kenagh / Foigha, and later in Killashee and Cloondra, which presented a problem for us as to how we could raise enough money to support them all.

A casual chat over a pint with Billy Henshaw, a life-long waterway enthusiast with a keen interest in the Royal Canal, spawned the idea of running a series of musical fundraising events for each RCAG branch. We would do an event at "home" in Athlone, where the branch members would travel, and then an "away" event where we would travel to each RCAG branch. These could be run through the 'off' season months from November to April. The raffle proceeds from each "home and away" event would go to that RCAG branch, and would be sufficient to pay their insurance bill for the year. Billy, a well-known entertainer, had vast experience in organising these types of events for all sorts of clubs, charities etc, and Billy had probably raised more aid money than Bob Geldof over the years. That was it, the decision was made – Billy organised a band, and Noel Duffy's Lough Ree Inn was booked for Saturday 8th May 1993, a host of willing volunteers collected spot prizes for the raffle, made sandwiches, sold tickets, and canvassed support for the night. Kenagh/Foigha branch arrived by bus and along with the locals had a great night of singing & dancing to Billy's band – Billy and his sons Billy jnr. and David, and

Larry Benson. As the song goes "the crowd called out for more", and a return night in Kenagh was arranged, – another great success and as a result, Kenagh/Foigha's funds for the year were much healthier. The band never charged for playing, and all the raffle prizes were sponsored, which meant that all the money raised went towards the RCAG branch funds. The name "The Royal Canal Band" was coined one night in Coosan and so it remained for the twelve years that the band existed. Soon after that Michael Martin and Joe Lacken joined the band, and these six musicians were the core of the Royal Canal Band since 1993, and since I myself couldn't sing for nuts they made me the manager! More recently Ted Quinn and Concepta Henshaw joined and became regular members of the band.

As the good word spread, other RCAG branches in Ballymahon, Abbeyshrule, Ballynacarrigy, Cloondara, became involved and a series of "home and away" music nights became the programme each year from November to May. The simple format of "easy on the ear" music from the band, a light hearted talent competition and an old time waltz competition for the audience, adjudicated by no less than a "Bachelor of Music", as Billy said "with letters after his name", but who shall be nameless, for fear of losing his customers or worse, having his credentials & parentage disputed, – such was the intensity of the competition!

Two raffles were run at each event with loads of prizes. The committees provided lots of sandwiches and cocktail sausages to be washed down with whatever you're having yourself! All contributed to a great night of entertainment which served not only to help with the funds for the RCAG branches but also strengthened the bond of friendship and support between the RCAG and the IWAI.

Over the years the band has been supplemented mainly by the Henshaw family – Tony, Marc, Sadie & Jim Byrne, and even a third generation of Henshaws, including Robbie, then a boy – now a rugby star with Connaught and Ireland, along with a host of guest artists – Frank Reid, Noel Breen, Sam Herraghty, Flan Barnwell, Pauline Downey, Paul Fogarty, Bill Dooley, and many more. All of these musicians together with the willing volunteers who provided food, sponsor prizes, sold tickets, and supported the functions, are to be complimented for the success of the musical nights. Probably the band's most important and memorable gig was for the Closing Dinner Dance in the Rustic Inn in Abbeyshrule for the Royal Canal Millennium Rally. A big hall, big stage, huge crowd, and the challenge of playing a dance routine rather than their usual sing-along routine in the cosy confines of a pub, but, fair play to them, they pulled it off and the night was a resounding success, they got great satisfaction from that. The humour on the bus to and from the venues and on stage, the craic and rivalry in the competitions, the hospitality and support they received everywhere, and the satisfaction of doing something worthwhile gave the band their greatest reward, and we thank them for the great memories.

It was my very great privilege to have been a part of it, and to have the Band playing The Auld Triangle on board Sakeena for the Opening Day parade into Richmond Harbour in October 2010 – Next stop – Longford!

Damien Delaney

Top Left; Royal Canal exiting Dublin with Croke Park in the background.

Bottom left; Abbeyshrule from the re aligned bridge over the Royal Canal

Top Right; The Royal Canal Band on board 'Sakeena'

Bottom Right; One of the new lifting bridges at the western end of the Royal.

91

Athlone Branch

Damien Delaney

The bridge at Athlone

A month after the formation of the IWAI the Athlone branch was formed on 19 February 1954 at a public meeting in the Cresent Ballroom Athlone. The first officers of the branch elected were

Chairman W.A. Tormey

Honorary Secretary T.A. Marrinan

Honorary Treasurer C. Rice

Committee Fr. Moran, D. Lyster, Mrs J. Reid, Dr J. O Meara, J. Newell, J. Glennon, P.J. Lynott, P.C. Molloy, T. Gallagher, T. Hoggan, A. Fadden, H. Waters, J. Wheatley, J. Williams, P. Hanley

Delegate Members: K. Kenny (Banagher), J O. Callaghan (Boyle)

Projects put forward were:

a) The maintenance of a swivel bridge at Athlone.

b) Feasibility of establishing a holiday camp on one of the larger islands of Lough Ree.

c) The providing of landing stages at well known local beauty spots and at historical places on the Shannon.

d) Reduction of freight charges on our canal systems.

e) That a boat slip be erected at Burgess Park.

f) That the reclaimed land in the vicinity of the River Shannon by Messrs Gentex Ltd be cleaned up.

g) Deputation to Westmeath County Council to have Sandy Bay re-opened to the general public.

h) Letter to Westmeath County Council regarding the deplorable condition of the Ballyglass and Coosan roads.

i) To investigate the possibility of the carriage of heavy building materials by water from Limerick to Athlone and important other centres.

j) To plant trees on the lower bank of the River Shannon.

Mr Sean McBride proposed that the views of the meeting, especially the condition of the Clarendon Lock at Knockvicar, be conveyed to those with re-

Sean McBride addresses an early IWAI meeting.

sponsibility for their upkeep – the lock was re-paired and re-opened to boating traffic in 1956.

Plans were made for a rally to the North Shannon and in 1954 two cruises were organized to Lanesboro and Clonmacnoise and in 1955 a number of open boats travelled to Knockvicar. At that time the lock was inoperative and participants had to haul the boats over the weir to continue their journey to Lough Key and Doon. By 1956 the Clarendon Lock at Knockvicar was re-opened and the way was clear for the first Shannon Boat Rally, Colonel Harry Rice acted as Commodore and travelled by open boat to Carrick-on-Shannon. The branch has continued the tradition of work parties and has completed and maintained a number of important sites around the

South Shannon. They have planted over six hundred trees, saved the trees on Carberry Island from damage, Mucknagh Wood trees at Lecarrow, installed seven safe anchorages on Lough Ree creating a safe ancorage from foul weather, also a clean-up of Rindoon Castle and maintained Ballykeeran jetty and much, much more.

The branch was actively involved in the prolonged campaign against the closing of the Grand and Royal canals. At a general meeting in May 1958 the following resolution was adopted "That this general meeting views with grave concern the provision in the proposed Transport Act 1958, now before the Dail whereby CIE is to be given the power to close any Irish Canal or Navigation under its control without further enquiry". The campaign was taken to every political party involved and, as a result of the efforts of the branch, the Bill was amended. The branch assisted other branches with other campaigns they fought, especially the proposed closure of the canals in Dublin to relieve the metropolitan traffic problem. It was not until 1964 that it was officially stated that the canals would not be closed.

In 1960 the branch set up a junior branch and at one stage had fifty-one junior members, sadly attendances fell away and the junior branch was disbanded in 1962.

The Athlone Aerial, a branch newsletter was introduced in 1975 and is still used to communicate branch policy and activities as well as other local

Athlone Town Marina.

marine club news, offers on chandlery and boating tips and is still produced today.

Vandalism was an issue on the River during the late seventies. The branch formed a sub-committee and with wide consultation with local traders, chamber of commerce, Gardai, Councillors, Board Failte, IBRA they developed a proposal to appoint a River Information Officer. The branch met with the County manager and other interested parties and the result was the appointment of the first River Warden in May 1978 with a view to solving the vandalism problem.

In recent years the branch has worked jointly with local organisations in bringing water projects to fruition such as the Athlone Canal, and provided financial support to Athlone Sub Aqua training room, maintained Dunrovin, the home of Colonel Harry and Cynthia Rice, the association's found-

ing members, erected a commerative sculpture at the town marina, launched a new branch burgee, run many cruise in companies, lobbied local government on many issues, the organisation of the RNLI rescue service for the South Shannon, the continued participation in the Shannon Rally and many more activities; all evidence of a busy organization.

Barrow Branch
John Dimond

I have tried (and failed) to get a paper trail or confirmed history of the Barrow Branch, even hearsay of the past is not to be had, sadly I cannot confirm the founding members of the branch.

Some say it was John Monaghan on coming from Canada to settle in Carlow and Bertie Shirley while Bill Duggan got involved later; but for those who don't know any better we might get away with either theory.

The Barrow Branch was one of the first five branches to be formed as part of IWAI; when in 1955 in Carlow the original Barrow Boys, Bill Duggan John Monaghan and Bertie Shirley started the campaign to ensure the Barrow Navigation remained in working order as CIE seemed to have lost interest as commercial traffic had already ceased.

Bill Duggan, a solicitor in Carlow restarted the Carlow Rowing Club. William L Duggan was recognised as being a particularly fine district court practitioner and was in his day actively involved with Carlow Rowing Club, Carlow Little Theatre

Memorial to Bertie Shirley and Bill Duggan.

and Co. Carlow Football Club; sadly William L Duggan died in 1991. Bill had a great love of the river Barrow and drew up the first navigation maps that are still used by those who boat on her silvery waters.

Bertie Shirley, who also was from Carlow, was a garage owner who started Barrow Line Holiday Cruisers Ltd. Bertie's boats were specially adapted for the testing conditions of the Barrow at that time. John Monaghan came from Canada and was a contributor for the *Farmers' Journal*. The men

worked tirelessly to ensure the Barrow remained navigable; indeed Bill Duggan was known to drive to Dublin to take up issues with CIE when anything detrimental was reported to him from his contacts all along the waterway. Today's *Barrow Guide* is based on the original notes compiled by Bill Duggan who prepared the charts of the navigation including cruising the rivers Nore and Suir at the low tide in order to mark the channel accurately.

Bill Duggan and John Monaghan both purchased Albin 25 motor cruisers in the early 70s and were seen cruising the navigation and the estuary in company. The branch started off events each year with an Easter Rally held anywhere between Bahanna Wood near St. Mullins on the south end of the Navigation up to Vicarstown in the North. Mrs Sadie Jefferson of Carlow was one of the early secretaries of the Barrow Branch and Ted Ray of Bagnelstown was also an active participant. Tom Connery, who was staying with Shirleys in the 70s, was introduced to the Barrow and to the IWAI; he along with Bertie's son Jimmy, cruised the waterway in "Coleen Bawn" one of the Barrow Line Holiday Cruisers. Bill Duggan remained an active IWAI member and the Branch President up until his death in 1991. Arthur Keppel became assistant Secretary and was also Treasurer in 1986 while Dr. Dermot Murphy became an active member in the mid 80s; he became the second President of the Branch on the death of Bill Duggan. When The Doc. Murphy died in 1993, Arthur Keppel became President, a role he holds today.

The Grannagh Boat Club members were involved towards the end of the 70s in the Barrow branch activity; here the main members were Dave Purcell and Michael Power. The Branch held only one meeting per year, that was the AGM, it was held at Carlow Boat club, later the meetings were held in the Leinster Hotel, Bagenalstown and then at the end of the 80s monthly meetings were held in Graiguenamanagh firstly in the Anchor Hotel, and when that closed the branch meetings moved to Doyle's Pub where they still take place.

Barrow Branch IWAI was instrumental in the setting up of the Barrow Award Scheme first run in 1971. This scheme changed the focus of the towns and villages, which until that time had their backs to the river; they were urged to see the waterway as the great asset that was flowing through their area. The Barrow awards continue to encourage local residents to take pride in their water frontage. One of the first major branch promotions of the Barrow took place when 1983 was declared, "The Year of the Barrow" ; this saw a large fleet of boats come down the navigation and cruise the estuary, the commodore for that event was Fr. Paddy Dowling. The next promotion was in '93 and was to visit 'The Three Sisters' the rivers, Nore, Suir and Barrow; this event saw over thirty boats in Kilkenny City to highlight the call to re-open the Kilkenny Canal and a full cruising programme was organised.

The second year of the Barrow was held in 2007, this got off to a high profile start with the President

The Dunbrody, a replica Famine Ship

of Ireland, Mary McAleese launching the programme on board the "Dunbrody", the tall-ship berthed in New Ross.

Belturbet Branch

Cathal Kinney

The Branch at Belturbet (Beal Tairbet – at the mouth of the Tairbet river) was formed in 1966 by noble gentlemen Barham, Brady, Doherty and Kenny. From the banks of the River Erne, which rises many miles away in south Cavan, you can travel some forty miles almost to the Atlantic Ocean ending a little inland at Belleek, indeed many a great cruise has been made over the decades since the formation of the Branch. In the

Belturbet branch members joining with Erne branch for rally.

the riverside enjoyable for those who simply want to relax with a stroll along the banks, stopping to take a breath at its beautiful marble Memorial Table and cobbled area with the more recent picnic seating amenity at the Ducking Stool. The first job for this project was to construct a jetty. This initial project was eventually turned into a more robust piece of engineering by the Branch in 2004, and in 2012 the Branch added new cleats to augment the old mooring rings on the sides of the steel girder and timbers.

Beturbet has always enjoyed the buzz of boating on its waters – from the gentle paddle of the rowing club, to the purr of motor-craft at Book-a-Boat in the 1960s, to the finery of Emerald Star in the 1990s.

From the start, the restoration of the Ballinamore-Ballyconnell Canal and complementary work on

1960s there was no navigation authority on the Upper River Erne so the Branch was mainly occupied with placing markers for navigation and building a jetty at the Ducking Stool close to the town. Over the years, stalwarts including current Branch President, Gerald Mackeral, IWAI Past President (1996) Liam D'Arcy, and current Vice-Chairman Charlie McGettigan have played an enormous part in keeping things afloat. Over many years those in the Belturbet Navy as they have been fondly described, have made their mark on the rivers and loughs of Cavan and Fermanagh. Then, as now, the main event in the calendar of activities has been the Lough Erne Boat Rally, which in 2014 will be led by Commodore Cathal Kinney, who has also been Branch Chairman for many years.

Belturbet is not just about boats and boaters, as the Branch has played a pivotal role in making

The spectacular Lough Oughter Castle on the upper stretches of the Erne system

the Woodford River at Corraquill (Lock No 1) and onwards to Ballyconnell, giving access to the Shannon was a possibility, and this was realised with the opening of the canal in 1994 with a rally where joint Commodores Gerald Mackeral and Kieran Walsh represented the Erne and Shannon areas respectively.

Today the Branch has a very active calendar of events from Easter time right through to Christmas. Current members come from North, South, East and West of the country, with quite a number of overseas members joining. Looking to the future, Belturbet members hope to see the construction of a new town jetty, which will provide one of the longest stretches of mooring anywhere in Ireland coupled with a long awaited Service Block. Of course we are right behind medium-term plans to see the re-opening of the Ulster Canal, and the somewhat longer-term the extension of the navigation beyond the town bridge at Belturbet up to Lough Oughter.

"Come listen to me, I've a story to tell
It's all about some people that you know quite well,
Down on the river on the boats they go,
I'll start with someone that I think you'll know".
With my too raa raa, fal da didle
daa, too raa roo raa roor raa ra

(From the Rally Song by Cathal Kinney, 2008)

Boyle River Branch

Peter Griffen

Members of the Boyle River branch

The Boyle River Branch has its origins in the foundation of the Cootehall Mariners Club, which held its inaugural meeting on the 18th January 2007 in the Cootehall Bridge Restaurant. The founding members were Catriona Gately, Paddy Gillboy, Alan Simon, Kevin Doherty, Michael Oates, Bearach Doherty, Jim and Maura Kelly, Peter and Ann Griffin, David and Laureen O'Dowd, Ray Devine, Trevor McDermott, Eric and Heidi Cahill and Ann and Dermot Cox. During the meeting the following were nominated and accepted as officers of the club; Commodore: David O'Dowd, Vice Commodore: Peter Griffin, Rear Commodore: Paddy Gilboy, Secretary: Ann

Castle Island

together to promote the well being of the local waterways.

Following a year of cruise activities, and an AGM vote to join the IWAI, the Cootehall Mariners Club met at the Royal Hotel in Boyle on 21st January 2008, to hold the inaugural meeting of the Boyle River Branch of the IWAI. This was attended by; Jackie Harvey, Declan Phelan, Joan Phelan, James Candon, Francis McGlynn, Peter Carroll, John Conlon, John Keeneghan, John Gallagher, John Murray, Tommy Egan, Sean Kenny, James Egan, Frank Feighan, Jim Feighan, Mary Martin, Eugene Coleman, Jim Ferrick, Michael O'Reilly, Jim O'Connell, Cathal McGee, Gerry Matimoe, Austin Mullarkey, Maura Doherty, Rory Martin, Alan Simon, Trevor McDermott, Laureen O'Dowd, David O'Dowd and Tommy Egan. The officers of the branch were elected as follows; Tommy Egan, Chairman; David O'Dowd, Vice Chairman; Peter Carroll, Treasurer and Peter Griffin, Secretary. A number of the members agreed on the evening to contribute to a founders' fund to facilitate the initial expenditure of the club. Paul Garland once again attended this inaugural meeting and gave a well received talk on the activities of the IWAI with an emphasis on boat safety and training of crew. Paul Garland concluded by formally presenting the IWAI burgee to Tommy Egan in recognition of the founding of the Boyle River Branch.

Since then membership of the branch has fluctuated going with current membership standing

Griffin, Membership Secretary: Ann Cox and Treasurer: Jim Kelly. Paul Garland was the invited guest and he provided an overview of the IWAI before taking questions on the pros and cons of joining the association. The meeting recognised the benefits of joining the IWAI, particularly from an insurance perspective, but decided to remain independent and review the situation in a years' time at the AGM. Subsequent correspondence from Paul Garland revealed that the Lough Key Boat Club was looking to become a branch of the IWAI in the future and consequently they agreed to join forces with the Cootehall Mariners Club. In September 2007 David O'Dowd and Ray Devine met with the chair and committee members of the Carrick branch to seek their views on the proposed Boyle River Branch. The case was made for having a separate Boyle river entity on geographical and historical grounds and agreement was reached that both Branches would work at 48. Sadly 2 of the founding members, Peter Carroll and Sean Kenny, passed away in 2011 and are sorely missed.

2013 has seen the branch starting a campaign to re-open the canal at Drumman's Island, Lough Key Forest Park for navigation by small leisure craft and lake day boats, and to reinstate the adjacent towpath for walkers. With resources restricted we recognise that this will be a major challenge, but we believe it to be a worthwhile project and will do all that we can to progress it.

Boyne Navigation branch workday

Boyne Navigation Branch

Myles Brady

Establishment of the Boyne Navigation Branch, IWAI was ratified by the Council of the IWAI as a branch of the Inland Waterways Association of Ireland at the Council meeting on Saturday, 19th May 2007. The primary objective of the Branch was continuation of early restoration work of the Boyne Navigation between Drogheda and Navan.

During the latter part of the last century, the Boyne Branch of the IWAI had been in existence and had carried out some initial clearance work on the sea-lock and other sections of the lower Navigation. However, due to lack of numbers and interest, the Branch went into decline, and finally closed in 1998; notable among those involved at

that time were Walter Ball, and the late Robert Law. Following branch closure, the responsibility for the work of the defunct Branch was assumed by the Dublin Branch at the request of the IWAI executive. One member of the original 'Boyne Branch' who maintained his branch subscription, despite closure of the branch, is Stephen Early, the present Water and Banks manager of the present Boyne Navigation Branch.

Myles takes a break due to blister injury!

Early in the year 2000 a group of mainly Dublin Branch members carried out occasional work parties along the navigation, and in April 2001 the First Boyne Dinghy Rally was held on the Navan canal section from Navan to Rowley's Lock. Again in April 2002 a small Boat Rally was organized on the Navan section. Two members of the present Boyne Navigation Branch who were heavily involved in this early activity were Seamus Costello, the present Branch Hon. Sec., and Padraig Costello, presently the mechanical plant manager. In 2003 it was decided to concentrate the restoration effort on the first canal section and the Sea-lock at Oldbridge, allowing progressive restoration from the tidal section of the navigation inland, and a subcommittee of mainly Dublin Branch members was formed. Involved at this stage were Derek Whelan, Mick Kinahan, Tommy McLoughlin with local councilor Frank Godfrey as chairman. This group was known locally as the Boyne Canal Action Group. Mike Egan, and Sophie Geraghty of the 'Lock Cottage' at Oldbridge sea-lock were also part of this group, and have remained enthusiastic backers of the restoration work, and Branch Members since branch inception. Several enthusiastic local volunteers together with the subcommittee members started restoration of this section by clearing a major buildup of debris allowing several very successful 'Open Days' to be organized.

In April 2006 this subcommittee was re-organized into a branch and renamed the Boyne Navigation Restoration Group with the intention of giving it responsibility for the long term restoration of the whole Navigation. On Tuesday, 24th April 2007,

the Boyne Navigation Restoration Group, with the enthusiastic agreement of the Dublin Branch Committee, met the IWAI Executive, at its meeting in Malahide Yacht Club and presented the case for establishment of the Boyne Navigation Branch, fully independent of the Dublin Branch, subsequently establishment of the new branch was ratified by Council. At the inaugural meeting of the new branch, it was agreed that the members of the committee of the Boyne Navigation Restoration Group would remain in office as the committee of the new branch for eighteen months.

The first AGM of the new branch was held on Tuesday, 4th Dec. 2007 and the first election of Officers and Committee was held at the second AGM, on Tuesday, 2nd Dec. 2008. The election of officers resulted in: Myles Brady, Chairman; Tommy McLoughlin, Vice Chairman; Sophie Geraghty, Hon Secretary, and John Martin as Treasurer.

One of the first tasks of the new Committee was to formalize the relationship between An Taisce, the owners of the Rights of the Navigation and the IWAI. Following lengthy negotiations, a formal agreement between the parties was finally signed on 23rd September 2010 recognizing the IWAI and the Boyne Navigation Branch, as exclusive agents of An Taisce in the restoration of the Boyne Navigation.

The main restoration work of the Branch since 2007 has focused on clearance of the Oldbridge

Canal section, and restoration of the Oldbridge sea-lock. This work involved clearance of the lock, rebuilding of the lock walls, fabrication and installation of breast and tail-gates, and paving and landscaping of the area. This work finally culminated in the re-opening of the sea-lock, connecting the tidal section of the river Boyne to the first canal section on the Navigation in Sept. 2013. Most of the finance for this work came from Meath Community, and Meath Heritage grants, together with significant support from local businesses in the form of finance and equipment loan support.

During 2013, work has also started on clearance of the river towpath and clearance of the lock at Stalleen Lower on the next canal section. Clearance work has also been carried out on a section of the canal at Athlumney, downstream from Navan, facilitating fishing for the first time on this section of the Navigation, and initial planning of restoration of the Slane Canal section is presently in progress.

Carrick-on-Shannon Branch
Conor Meegan

The inaugural meeting of the Carrick-on-Shannon branch took place on Thursday November 11th 1954 in the town hall with Thomas Burke presiding; this initial meeting was to sow the seed of what has become the largest branch in the Association.

Carrick-on-Shannon boat club

The initial executive comprised of local business people, clergy and members of the local boating community. As one of the founding branches of this new association Carrick-on-Shannon branch were quick to realise the potential of securing and preserving the existing navigation but also that by providing and improving facilities on the north Shannon the benefits it would bring to the area.

In 1955 this active committee made representations to national bodies such as ESB, CIE and the Board of works with regard to sluices being repaired and monitored to keep levels at a level suitable for all craft thus increasing commercial traffic and facilitating the new CIE hotel barges and leisure boats to the area.

By April 1956 branch records show significant improvements to the navigation including the retention of the bridge in Lanesboro, navigation markers along the river and mooring buoys installed at various locations, a boatbuilding class was also initiated in the town of Carrick at the behest of branch recommendations.

By 1960 the quay area in Carrick had also seen improvements such as mooring chains and tyres fitted to the quay wall, litter bins, the first dedicated water supply tap and a phone box all initiated by the branch for the benefit of visiting boaters, also at this time the branch proposed the construction of a slipway at the "cattlepass" on the Roscommon side of the river at a cost of £50.00 which is still in place to this day.

The branch was growing and the amalgamation with the Carrick yacht club bolstered the branch and its position in the community. By this time some of the now well-known names associated with the early years were emerging, the likes of Tom Maher, Bill Child, Doc Farrell, stalwarts of the branch for many years to come. Along with the on-going work there was also some fun and cruise in company, curry nights and film shows were a regular of the social calendar.

The first mention of the Shannon Boat Rally was in 1961 with arrangements made for berthing and the promise of light refreshments provided for all participants in the Bush hotel. This is a tradition that continues to this day with the Bush hotel still welcoming the rally year after year.

By now Carrick-on-Shannon had earned the name as the "Friendly branch" as visiting boaters were welcomed to the town personally each day by branch members and facilities such as laundry and bathing, fuel and grocery delivery were offered locally to any one requiring them.

By 1965 records show the passage of vessels though Albert lock and visiting Carrick had increased 100% year on year. While continuously making improvements to the area the branch facilitated work to Clarendon lock with the placing of new benches and planters, which were transported by barge from Carrick by John Weaving who was now an active branch member.

By the early 1970s the branch was now well established as one of the largest memberships, with regular meetings and work parties, working closely with the Board of works and Bord Failte; the profile of Carrick-on-Shannon continued to rise. Now a popular tourist destination with several hire companies such as Flagline, Emerald star, Carrick Craft and Mitchell marine provide boat hire and services to the boating community.

Coalisland Branch

Thomas McIlvenna.

The Coalisland Canal Branch is a unique organisation in some respects, one of the more noticeable facts is that every enthusiastic member has

The late Jim Canning, Father figure of the Coalisland branch

access to navigable water in almost every direction in which he or she looks, but none of them possess a boat of any kind! The reasons for this and other anomalies emanate from the rich historical tapestry of this East Tyrone town.

At the start of the recent "Troubles", events in and around Coalisland reflected so exactly the wider ensuing tragedy throughout the country that "the Island" became a microcosm of Northern Ireland as a whole. The 1830's industrial landscape, described by Dr. Michael Dillon, had collapsed into a desert of despair. The famous area around the Basin, which was part of the first inter-connecting inland waterway system in Ireland or Britain, rapidly lost its factories, brick and pipe works, mines, sandpits, engineering sheds, mills and small businesses. The canal and railway had long since ceased to operate. Local man, Frank O'Neill's satirical song, Filling in the Basin, took on an ironic and slightly bitter tinge.

Oh, they're filling in the Basin and my
heart is full of woe,
No more I'll see the golden sands when
the tides are running low.
No more the salty breezes will be wafted up the hill,
Or mighty breakers bash against
the ramparts of the mill.

The Quay, Coalisland

However, in the face of all the devastation and depression the entrepreneurial spirit which had founded Coalisland and had maintained it through lean times in the past was reasserted by the local Development Association in a drive aimed at restoring the self-esteem of this unusual industrial enclave in East Tyrone. A fitting first step was the opening of the modest Canal Basin Park in November 1975 on a small portion of the Tyrone Navigation in-filled terminus. Several local people helped to bring the project to fruition but the driving force for it and the subsequent transformation of much of the town was Councillor Jim Canning.

By February 1981 the Coalisland and District Development Association, once again vigorously encouraged by Jim, set up a sound commercial base for small enterprises and the training of young people in a wide range of skills. As the signs of improvement became more and more visible,

"The Point" where the Coalisland Canal leaves the Blackwater

recommended but this didn't satisfy Jim Canning or the growing number of supporters of his regeneration plans. These, "Friends of the Coalisland Canal", were heartened, however, by the award of a colossal £2.7 million from the Community Regeneration and Special Projects (C.R.I.S.P.) fund in September 1990 to the Development Association. As the finishing touches were laid to the magnificently refurbished Corn Mill Heritage Centre, Jim Canning made it clear that the next step had to be the canal.

Supporters from far and near joined in all sorts of awareness-raising ventures – lectures, concerts and canal walks. Eventually, Brian Cassells, then Vice-President of the I.A.W.I., Victor Hamill, Chairman of the River Bann and Lough Neagh Association with his wife, Jacqueline, and Michael Savage advised a meeting of canal supporters to form themselves into a branch of the I.W.A.I. in May 2003. Thus the most unusual inland waterways group came into being, the town and community which had been created by the canal was giving something back in an attempt to preserve and regenerate a valuable economic resource. The high profile of the group was maintained by activities such as, The Small Boat Rally of 2004, organised by Ken and Jane Bell with Hugh King. Members were also treated to an enjoyable day's cruising by the Lough Erne boating fraternity in June 2004. The society even published its own book entitled, *This Wonder-Working Canal*, by Thomas McIlvenna.

the obvious next move was to demolish Stewarts Mill, a rat-infested shell of a derelict grain mill, a dangerous eyesore towering over the very centre of the town. To everyone's astonishment Jim Canning opposed the move and through his integrity and vision convinced the people that, "The Mill", should be saved and transformed into a heritage centre standing in the re-opened Basin of a new Coalisland Canal, stretching once more to, "The Point", on the River Blackwater where it had all begun in 1733. With some people who had vociferously campaigned for the bulldozing of Stewarts Mill now actively supporting the councillor, the local authorities in Dungannon commissioned a feasibility survey on the canal which was by now only a drainage ditch – maybe the longest overflow channel in Ireland – but still only a ditch. An elaborate cosmetic scheme was all that could be

Sadly, Jim Canning did not live to see the re-opening of the Coalisland Canal nor did his associate, honorary branch secretary Johnny Cavanagh, Norman Badger nor Gabrielle Daly. Nevertheless, their vision lives on and in better times to come will be continued and achieve success for the I.W.A.I. Coalisland Canal Branch. Once again we shall be able to sing the old traditional rhyme:

Belfast can boast of its harbour,
Dublin can boast of its quay,
But Coalisland can boast of her Basin
Where the boats come and go every day.

Lough Corrib

Corrib Branch

Michael J Hynes

The genesis of the IWAI Corrib Branch was a visit by Christy Deacy and Gerry Glynn to an IWAI meeting on a barge called "Ye Iron Lung" (formerly 49M) moored in Athlone back in 1976. They returned enthused by what they had seen and set up the Corrib Branch of IWAI. Gerry Glynn was the first Chairman (called President at that time) and David Baynes was the first secretary.

The first rally was held in 1976. It started in Kilbeg with a small number of boats and a number of people camping on the pier. The next recorded rally was in 1978. It is well remembered by those who participated as the weather was atrocious and resulted in the loss of the famous "Pelican" owned

by Christy Deacy. That particular rally went to Maam Bridge, a habit that has lasted to this day.

Unlike the Shannon, the Corrib had a relatively poor infrastructure from a cruising point of view at that time and the Corrib Branch went about rectifying this deficiency. A new pier was constructed in Inchagoill in 1991 and it is usually full during the summer weekends. The construction of this pier was a major logistics exercise as all the materials had to be ferried from the mainland in relatively small craft. Christy Deacy oversaw much of this project with his usual enthusiasm. I am led to believe that a heavily laden boat owned by Pat McCambridge sank during the trip between Cong and Inchagoill and to this day has not been located. Perhaps someone one day will find it with modern echo sounding sonar equipment. Apart from Lisloughrey Pier where many of the Corrib Branch members have moorings, this pier is by

A contemplative Christy Deacy, father figure of the Corrib

far the most widely used by the cruising fraternity.

During the winter of 1992 and spring of 1993 a new pier was constructed at Maam Bridge. While still a major engineering project, it was a simpler exercise than the Inchagoill project as materials and equipment could be readily transported by truck. Again, Christy Deacy was the driving force behind this project. The official opening of this pier was performed by President Mary Robinson in July 1993. She was carried from Cornamona to and up the river in Paul & Susan Horan's magnificent "Soliman Buffoen", colloquially known as Soliman B. This 13.2 x 3.65 x 1 m craft is the largest cruiser on the Corrib and was built in Belgium in 1898. A plaque honouring Christy Deacy's contribution to the Maam Bridge pier project is located near the pier. It reads:

Inland Waters Association of Ireland Lough Corrib Branch Dedicates this Plaque to the Memory of Christy Deacy 1947 – 2003.

In the early days, boats were relatively small and for many participants, the rallies were a combination of boating and camping. For example there were two Manta 19s (Peadar Canavan and Joe Curley) and one Manta 16 (Pete Smith) on the 1979 rally – this rally was also accompanied by high winds. Other members on this rally included Adrian Ryder, Pat Higgins, George Ryder and Pat McCambridge.

Traditionally, there have been two rallies on the Corrib every year. The summer rally takes place over three days on the second weekend of July while the autumn rally takes place on the second weekend of September. Other events are also organised including the opening barbecue of the season on Lisloughrey pier in early May, a children's event and a mid-summer gathering to celebrate the longest day of the year. Over the year, many rally routes have been utilised. Piers visited include Kilbeg, Knockferry, Oughterard, Cornamona, Maam Bridge, the marina adjacent to Macs pub in Cornamona (now closed and sadly missed) and of course the pier at Inchagoill and the pontoon in Cleenillaun.

Former Chairmen include Chris Crowley (who was Chairman and Commodore for many years), Glenn Ryder, Jimmo Kelly, Ger O'Máille, George Ryder, Sean Heavey, Liam Madden, Pat McCambridge, Peadar Canavan and Noel Flynn. The current Chairman is Michael J. Hynes. Secretaries included Shiela Baynes, Mary Canavan, Ann O'Máille and Zara Brady, the current Secretary.

As with many IWAI branches, membership of the Corrib Branch fluctuates and has never exceeded the magic one hundred mark. To a certain extent this is a result of the relatively poor facilities on the Corrib compared to the Shannon. Moorings in Lisloughrey Harbour are as scarce as hens' teeth and now new boat owners have no place to moor their boats. There are no marinas and as the whole of the Corrib is an SAC, it is going to be difficult to secure planning permission for any such developments. Indeed many members are also members of the Corrib Rowing and Yachting Club in Galway which has berthing and hard-stand facilities.

Navigation on the Corrib is controlled by the Corrib Navigation Trustees and unlike Waterways Ireland; their remit is strictly limited to navigation issues and maintenance of piers at Kilbeg, Knockferry and Lisloughrey. Over the past year the 'old' non-standard navigation marks have been replaced by new marks which comply with the IALA system. This has been a long time coming and the author first wrote to the Trustees back in 1982 recommending that they implement such a system. Modern charts containing all the marks are now available from www.anglingcharts.com and as a result, navigation on the Corrib is now much safer.

Cruising Club Branch

Paul J Scannell,

Inaugural meeting of the Cruising Club

The concept of the Cruising Club was conceived by Maurice Kerr in 2006 and formally came to fruition on 21st April 2007 at an inaugural meeting held in Killaloe. At that meeting the following Club Officers were elected: Chairman: Maurice Kerr; Vice-Chairman: Paul Scannell; Secretary: Derry Smyth; Treasurer: Joe O'Dubhghaill; Safety Officer: John Ryan; Council Rep: Sean O'Riogain; IWN Rep: Tricia Kerr; Webmaster: Paul Scannell; Child Protection Officer: Lorna Wynne

The club was officially sanctioned as a branch of the IWAI at its Council meeting on 19th May 2007. The first formal meeting of the new branch took place on the 26th May 2007 at the Shannon Oaks Hotel, Portumna. The meeting drew an at-

In harbour

tendance of approximately 30 members including Brian Cassells, IWAI President at that time, who had been an early supporter of the fledgling branch.

The Cruising Club was a unique addition to the IWAI family in so far as it was the first branch that was non-geographically based. The role of 'Commodore' (a position held for the season) was introduced in 2010 and the title-holder is expected to give assistance to the various Event Commodores (one per CIC) in respect of the planning and implementation of each event.

The club draws its membership from across the country and includes boat-owners with home berths stretching from Killaloe to Carrick-on-Shannon. It has also attracted overseas members who are domiciled in the UK, and USA.

By 2009 club membership had risen to 71 (50 family and 21 single) reflecting approximately 120 persons encompassing a fleet of close to 60 boats. At present the membership level stands at 54 (43 families and 11 single).

The primary activity of the branch was (and still is!) the organisation and implementation of Cruises-in-Company that usually took place over weekends. Cruising grounds include the entire length of navigable waterways stretching from Limerick to Lough Erne. The branch has also organised CICs to Kilrush and on the River Barrow. In recent years some members have participated in coastal cruising on the west and south-west coasts of Ireland.

Each year there is usually one lengthy CIC of at least 7 days duration. Previous destinations for such events have included: Kilrush, Lough Derg, Lough Ree, Carrick-on-Shannon and Lough Erne.

Heading down the estuary for Kilrush

Participation levels in regular club CICs range from 5 – 17 boats and such weekends typically incorporate a diverse range of activities including, inter-alia and in no particular order, some of the following: walks and guided tours, go-karting, dancing, BBQ's, pitch & putt, sing-songs, table quizzes, team sports, RIB/dinghy trips, educational/training courses. Also, in the early years, club meetings were often conducted during CIC weekends. The Cruising Club also organises joint activities with other branches. The club holds an AGM at the end of November, which is immediately followed by the annual club dinner on the same evening. The branch operates a website (www.cruising.iwai.ie) which hosts an extensive pictorial archive dating back to the foundation of the club.

Although a relatively young branch, the Cruising Club has seen several of its members serve at national level. These include: Derry Smyth who served as Hon. Secretary IWAI from 2010 – 2013 and was subsequently elected Vice-President of the national body at its AGM in April 2013. Joe O'Dubhghaill and Maurice Kerr also served as Directors of IWAI.

Although, according to membership numbers, the Cruising Club might not be regarded as a large branch, it has, over the relatively small number of years of its existence, established itself as an active and vibrant member of the IWAI community and has certainly lived up to its slogan… 'We're going places'.

Dublin Branch

Derek Whelan

The history of the Dublin Branch is closely bound up with the history of the IWAI as a national body. Many of the early founders were from the Dublin area. The organisation had come into being in the 1950s because of a perceived threat to the river Shannon but new threats caused attention to shift towards the capital city. In 1963 the then Dublin Corporation published a plan to install a major new sewer on the bed of the Grand Canal through the city. It was even suggested that the canal route might be converted to a motorway (though we hardly knew what a motorway was in those early days). A Dublin branch was formed in 1964 with a view to preventing this plan from becoming a reality.

Grand Canal Lock

Dublin canal-side

IWAI campaign against new bye-laws

What followed was a series of events to arouse public sympathy, lobbying of councillors and politicians up to government ministers, and even public protests. The campaign was successful and gave the branch the confidence to initiate a policy that has been upheld for the past 50 years.

That policy was; "To keep the canals of Dublin open to navigation for future generations."

In accordance with the policy of keeping the navigation through Dublin open, it had been decided to hold a Dublin Boat Rally annually and this tradition has been upheld for the past 30 years. A high point on this programme was reached in 1988 (The Millenium Year) when over 80 boats were locked through to the city over an 18-hour period. By now, control of inland waterways had passed from CIE to OPW and their assistance was vital to the success of the operation. Nevertheless, the input of the Dublin IWAI Committee to the success of that Rally was not fully acknowledged by the national media at the time.

The 50th anniversary of the founding of IWAI was celebrated with a 50/50 Rally in 2004 which succeeded in attracting over 50 boats to the city basin. In recent years it has become possible to welcome boats to the Dublin Rally through both canals – boaters from the North Shannon and Erne are now finding it easier to reach Dublin through the Royal Canal.

Since the Royal finally opened to the Shannon in 2010 and with an agreed schedule for the lifting of the Railway Bridge near Newcomen Bridge it has become possible to complete the "ring" for the first time since the famous 1955 Hark voyage.

The Dublin branch initiated a Green & Silver Challenge to encourage this traffic and over 80 boats have now completed the challenge and been awarded commemorative plaques and certificates.

Although planning the Dublin Rallies has been a major part of the work of the branch over the years it was just one of a number of events held every year. From the early days small boat events were held – sometimes these were referred to as "Dinghy Scrambles" and often included canoes (sometimes in cooperation with the Irish Canoe Union).

The highlight of the social calendar was the Annual Dinner Dance (which was held, usually, at the Court Hotel, Killiney) which attracted up to 150 people every year, many travelling from other IWAI branches around the country. Although the Dinner Dances (and the hotel) are now long past, mention of them will bring back very happy memories to many IWAI members from all across the country.

At the request of IWAI Council Dublin Branch undertook the organisation of the IWAI stand at the Dublin Boat Show which was held every second year up until 2008. The Stand was an important channel for signing-up new members to the organisation and in promoting the message of the association to the wider boating community.

Another highlight of recent years was the successful organisation (in association with Waterways Ireland) of the World Canal Conference held in Dublin in 2001, the only occasion when the

Sir Samuel Beckett Bridge

Conference was held in Ireland. Some of the American delegates were able to hire boats on the Royal Canal and travel by canal to attend the event.

The recent decade has seen a change in emphasis in how the Branch sees its future. Cooperation with other organisations from local authorities to local Community groups has been intensified through the Sub Groups of the Grand and Royal Canals and through the OLG (Operational Liaison Group), which has been active for the past 3 years. This has brought us into contact with new groups with which we can work to achieve better progress in the future. We have saved our waterways heritage in Dublin; now we need to use it.

Looking back over the records of the past 50 years one must be impressed by the passion and energy of the early pioneers of Dublin Branch. They achieved so much over a short period of time and changed official attitudes of indifference and neglect. Dublin Branch can look forward with confidence to the future for the waterways in the city. It may seem churlish not to mention names of members who have contributed significantly to 50 years of progress on the Dublin waterways but they are far too numerous to list here.

Happily, most of them are still with us and can celebrate our success on our 50th Birthday.

Foigha & Kenagh Branch

Gerry O'Hara

Mosstown Harbour

The inaugural meeting of the Foigha-Kenagh Canal Amenity Group was held in St. Dominic's Hall, Kenagh on the 20th March 1991.

The Committee persons elected were: Pat Newman, Michael Blaney, Bernie Mathews, Elspeth Hall and Maria McPhillips. The Committee in evaluating a works program towards the restoration found that the canal banks were severely overgrown, and the canal itself had dense vegetation in the shallow muddy water. Many years of neglect had taken their toll. Local opinion was that the canal could never be re-opened. Throughout Co. Longford six culverts had been built over the main line of the canal and it seemed that the money to replace them might be a major obstacle to complete the restoration. However, our little group were both dedicated and determined to achieve our goals.

Foigha-Kenagh Canal Amenity Group affiliated with the Royal Canal Amenity Group, which had been set up to work towards the complete restoration of the canal from Dublin to the Shannon. We were greatly encouraged by both Dr. Ian Bath and the late Eddie Slane. The first task was for the group to walk along the canal and become familiar with the area in order to plan where we might start. Following this the voluntary work parties began. Crowds met weekly to take ivy from the bridges, cut overhanging bushes and clear canal banks. These work parties were happy, sociable events and always ended with a cuppa and chat. Our first Fas Scheme started in August 1991 and with this regular work plus the voluntary support, large tracts of canal bank were quickly opened up. The Athlone Branch of the IWAI came and helped with the bank clearance.

Considerable funds were needed by the group to carry out the works whereby cake sales, raffles, bring and buy sales plus fund raising nights in Newman's pub, Kenagh became the norm. Again the Athlone Branch of the IWAI was very supportive of fund raising events and often organised events both in Coosan and Kenagh. It was with great delight that dredging was completed in the Foigha-Kenagh area by 1995 and the machines then moved on to Killashee. However, at this stage extensive weed growth remained in the canal and our group decided to purchase a weed cutting boat and cut back the weeds in 1996. Our beloved canal was at long last beginning to look like a canal.

Unfortunately years were to pass before the canal became navigable in our area. The biggest obstacle of all remained were the culverts across the canal. With six million of EU money the culverts were removed and new bridges built. Finally in 2009, the first boats for decades sailed into Foigha Harbour to join the local celebrations; however, it was to be a full year before the boats arrived in Mosstown Harbour. With the official opening of the canal in 2010, Foigha-Kenagh Canal Amenity Group could feel justifiably proud of their work over the previous nineteen years. The following year, 2011, we were to play host to the first official visiting rally from the Lough Erne Branch of the IWAI. Pat Newman was now to relive his experience at Foigha Harbour in 2009 when two years later he awaited the flotilla in Mosstown Harbour and give one and all a Royal welcome. The host-

Proceeding along the Royal Canal

ing of such an event was a major celebration and recognition of all the years of hard work, that now the Royal Canal was well and truly open. It furthermore created awareness as to the potential in establishing and consolidating an IWAI branch and be part of a progressive Inland Waterways Association.

Gerry O'Hara, Bernie Mathews and Pat Newman discussed and debated the way forward and were unanimous in applying for membership of the IWAI. Harry Hall came on board and the committee were adamant that the support and structure of the IWAI was vital in pursuing our goals and the future development of the potential branch. Contact was made with Dr. Ian Bath to seek his views and support for the application, and without hesitation he gave his endorsement. Application to join the IWAI was submitted in April 2013 and endorsed in June 2013 to form the 22nd branch of the Inland Waterways Association of Ireland on the 41st level of the Royal Canal.

Committee:
    President: Pat Newman
    Chairman: Gerry O'Hara
    Vice Chair: Bernie Mathews
    Secretary: Tony Moran
    Treasurer: Kieran McEntee
    PRO: Harry Hall

Installing new lock gates at 3rd lock on Naas branch

Kildare Branch

Beth O Loughlin

The Kildare Branch has evolved from 1975, when the North Kildare Branch covering the Sallins, Naas and Robertstown areas was formed, to 1984, when the official Kildare IWAI was established, encompassing all the waterways in Kildare. Kildare IWAI today, covers the waterways from Lock 12 at Newcastle Road to Lock 20 at Ticknevin on the Grand Canal Main Line, the Naas and Corbally Branches, the Milltown Feeder and south on the Barrow Line as far as Lock 22 at Glenaree. On the Royal Canal, the Branch has an interest from Confey near Leixlip west to Kilcock.

In the early days, Dublin members took an active interest in Kildare waterways. In 1973, the Dublin Branch organised trips on the City Line of the Grand Canal with one of the Robertstown

barges, carrying in total 1,383 passengers and in 1974 they organised a St Patrick's Day rally in Robertstown. Dublin Branch was still involved in 1977 when members carried out repairs to Lock 1 on the Naas Branch, the beginning of the restoration of this delightful stretch. In 1978 everyone got together to organise a rally on the Naas Branch and Lock 1 was brought into action for the first time in many years. The Naas Branch restoration was helped in 1979, when AnCo, a youth training and employment agency, set up a project to make lock gates for the Royal Canal and the Naas Branch of the Grand Canal, providing suitable premises could be obtained. 1980 saw a rally organised to focus attention on the restoration of the Naas Branch and later that year refurbishment work began at both ends. The following year the Minister for Transport, Albert Reynolds, inaugurated Lockgate AnCo, a scheme situated in premises made available by Messrs Arthur Guinness. In 1982 Dublin IWAI organised a work party at Lock 3 of the Naas Branch, extending the navigation further south. Naas Urban Council made money available for the timber needed to enable AnCo to make lock gates at the Watling Street premises. There were great celebrations in 1987 to mark the official re-opening of the Naas Branch of the Grand Canal Line, attended by the Minister for the Environment and a couple of years later, crowds of local people celebrated the 1989 Naas Harbour Festival. Kildare IWAI continues this tradition today with their annual autumn festival in the Harbour.

In recent years there has been great interest in restoring the Corbally Branch as far as Corbally Harbour. The Corbally Branch is the feeder for the Naas Branch, with water fed from the springs in Corbally Harbour through a large pipe under the old Limerick Road. The decision to build this culvert was made back in 1954, dividing the line and making it impassable to walkers, cyclists and boaters. Until recent years, there did not seem much hope of changing this disastrous decision, as the road was the major artery between Dublin and Limerick. However, now this has changed and Kildare IWAI is actively campaigning for the re-opening of the line. The concept is to have a Linear Park for local people and visitors that will allow all sorts of boats to travel the full length of the canal and to have a path and cycleway all along the edges, with resting places at one or two points along the way. All sorts of boats from 10 feet to 60 feet have travelled the stretch in recent years as far as the culvert.

Surveying the Corbally branch

Over on the Royal Canal in 1983 after a huge amount of effort by volunteers, the Kilcock Festival took place in a restored harbour and a re-watered level. There have been many events since along this Kildare stretch of the Royal. In 2001 the Irish International Canoe Polo Championships were held at Kilcock Harbour and in 2012 a contingent of Kildare boats having travelled from the Naas Branch, along the Grand Canal to Dublin, finally made their way into Kilcock Harbour.

Moving boats through locks continues to be one of the main aims of Kildare IWAI with boats attending rallies every year both in Kildare and all over the waterway system. Many Kildare boats travel to Dublin for the annual rally in May each year and were there in 2001 during the World Canal Conference. In 2004 all along the Grand

'Aqualegia' and 'Magnet 'moored at Leinster Mills on the Nass branch

Canal, we celebrated 50 years of the IWAI and 200 years of the Grand Canal with events in Dublin, Edenderry, Tullamore and Shannon Harbour. In 2009 the Branch welcomed the HBA to the Naas Harbour Festival, when for the first time in many years, a flotilla of Grand Canal Company and other heritage boats made their way through the five locks to Naas. As well as the spring events, Kildare has become known among the boating community for its end of season happening, when many boats travel back from their spring, summer and autumn cruising around the country to meet up again in Naas at the end of October. It may be a bit chilly outside but the warm welcome from the people of Naas, strange looking people in Halloween costumes and the boats lit up in the harbour and along the canal, make this weekend a great social occasion.

Lagan Branch

Jim Henning

The Lagan Navigation travels 27 miles east to west from Belfast Harbour to Lough Neagh and was one of the most successful commercial navigations in Ireland. Among its 27 locks it boasts the only flight of four locks (Union Locks Lisburn) on the Irish waterway network. It passes through four local Government Council areas – Belfast, Castlereagh, Lisburn and Craigavon and travels through three counties Antrim, Down and Armagh.

Lagan branch founder chairman Jim Henning with councillor Ruth Patterson

The Lagan Branch of the Inland Waterways Association of Ireland was formed on Thursday 20th January 2005 at a Public Meeting held in Lisburn Civic Centre. This meeting was promoted jointly by Lisburn City Council and IWAI to consider how a new IWAI branch could focus at-

On the Lagan

tention on the derelict Lagan navigation. The waterway enthusiasts attending with members of the public and totalling over 80 received presentations from Councillor Edwin Poots, Lisburn City Council, Brian Cassells the then Vice president of IWAI, Jim Canning chairman of the Coalisland branch of IWAI and Erskine Holmes, Ulster Waterways Group.

A discussion followed with everyone present supporting the formation of a new branch of IWAI and to be named the Lagan Branch.

Jim Henning MBE was elected chairman and Linda Crymble, Lagan Corridor Project Officer with Lisburn City Council was elected honorary secretary.

The aims of the new branch were to:-
- Promote the restoration, use and maintenance of the disused Lagan navigation.
- Lobby and advise Government and others on all matters connected with the Lagan waterway including pollution and future developments.
- Organise boat rallies and other events specific to the Lagan navigation.
- Organise work parties and raise funds to improve and restore the closed derelict sections of the Lagan navigation.

The first actual branch meeting took place on 17th February 2005 in Lisburn Island Centre where additional members were elected to the committee and a programme of events for the incoming year was discussed. The first event was to be a boat rally on the river Lagan on 16th April 2005 to raise public awareness of the need to have the Lagan navigation re-opened from Belfast Harbour to Lough Neagh, and to promote the newly formed branch of the Inland Waterways Association of Ireland.

The first Lagan boat rally was a great success with some 50 boats from all over Ireland taking part. This was the first time in over 50 years that so many boats were seen on the river Lagan and the Lagan branch, through this boat rally showcased their commitment to work towards the eventual restoration of this disused navigation.

Belfast City Council demonstrated their support to the Lagan branch of IWAI with requests and sponsorship for two further notable boat rallies', in May 2007 to mark the 10th Anniversary of

Lagan small boat rally

the opening of the Waterfront Hall, and again in August 2009 as part of the programme of events supporting the second visit of the Tall Ships to Belfast.

Canal restoration is an extremely slow process taking many decades to achieve, and to maintain the interest of the branch members a programme of monthly activities takes place year on year. These include walks, talks, visits, boat rallies, boat trips, presentations, work parties and meetings, and inviting other branch members to the Lagan branch events and taking part in other branch activities has been successful in maintaining membership and promoting the objectives of the Inland Waterways Association of Ireland.

The Lagan Navigation celebrated its 250th Birthday in September 2013 with a number of events organised by the Lagan Canal Trust and the Lagan branch of IWAI; one of the events was a "Party" at Union Locks. This important heritage site had become so overgrown that it was virtually hidden from view. Funding for shrub clearance and a complete survey of this scheduled monument was secured. Contractors removed larger trees and also removed many tons of sediment from all four lock chambers and carried out all the heavy site works.

Lagan branch members took part regularly in work parties for many months and along with members from Northern Ireland Conservation Volunteers clocked up more than 11,000 hours completing the work. A Conservation Management Plan is now in place for the entire site. This unique lock flight is now a nostalgic attraction to the many thousands of towpath users and tourists demonstrating the commitment that branch members have towards the eventual restoration of the Lagan navigation.

Lough Derg Branch
Natalie Magowan

IWAI Lough Derg branch's first meeting was held in Terryglass on the 10th October 1970. Although the main object of the association is to promote the restoration and maintenance of the inland waterways it was felt that Lough Derg Branch was justified in aiming also to promote the interests of

Dromineer

Holding the boat as it descends 60ft at the imposing Ardnacrusha lock

all boat users on the lake and at the same time safeguarding the amenities of the area. Main items for discussion in those early days still remain the same today, mainly concerns about pollution, marking of buoys, the confusing markers in middle ground and lack of toilet facilities. The membership fee in that first year was £1 with 25p due to council or as it was referred to as 'HQ' however this capitation fee was waivered for the first two years.

The branch's region covers the waterways from Victoria Lock at Meelick to the Sea Lock at Sarsfield Bridge. The main activity of the Lough Derg Branch is the week-long boat rally held in early July but the branch also holds regular branch meetings, work-parties, talks and discussions and cruises in company. Over the years the branch has also travelled to other waterways and participated in events with other branches; such as joining with the Shannon Rally for a Millennium Rally in 2000 and a memorable trip up north (2002) to enjoy the delights of Lough Neagh and the River Bann and in 2008 travelling west to Lough Corrib with its stunning scenery.

Trips through the double locks of Ardnacrusha, down the unpredictable Abbey River to Limerick marina have been undertaken by the branch on numerous occasions. In 1987 some members had the foresight to obtain permission from landowners up the Woodford River to moor along the banks. This led to a formal legal agreement granting the branch a lease for 99 years at the Conor Hogan Jetty, a perfect hideaway for members over the years. As the Woodford River is not part of the official navigation, branch members have to undertake the maintenance and this has given members the confidence to look at other navigations off the beaten track such as the Cappagh River, Black Lough and the Errina Canal.

Lough Erne Branch

John Suitor

Enniskillen Castle

Several boat owners on Lough Erne joined together to have an outing on the lake in the early 1960's. Due to its success they decided to form a branch of the I.W.A.I. and join with the Belturbet Branch to organise an annual boat rally after the style of the Shannon Rally. The first rally was held in 1966 the commodore being Peter Denham. The new branch was called the Enniskillen Branch.

Some of the founder branch members were -Hubert Brown, Ian Brown , Des Dolan, Eddie Hall, Conor Johnston , Mr. MacCrae Elliott, Jim Barkley, Wesley Dawson, Pat Maguiness, Colin Beattie, Albert Broomhead and Fred Johnston.

As no meetings or AGMs were held, the branch became dormant but the rally continued to be held. Some years later Des Dolan, the first branch secretary handed the minute book to John Suitor requesting him to get the branch reformed; together with Mike Gledhill they called a public meeting to achieve this. The branch was renamed the Lough Erne Branch, Mike Gledhill was elected chairman and John Suitor as secretary. Other members who later held the office of chairman were Ronnie Crawford, Jack Boland and Jeff Woolley while I.W.A.I. council meetings were attended by John Suitor. Florrie and Hubert Brown, who lived at Carrybridge had built a marina and they and the marina were the centre of branch activity for many members in the early years.

Newry and Portadown Branch

Geraldine Foley

The Newry & Portadown branch was formed in March 2005 at a very well attended public meeting in Newry. The first chairman was, appropriately, Rowan Hand who had played an important role in the Newry Canal Preservation Society, which had kept the canal safe from developers since the closure of the port of Newry in the 1970s. The branch in the early years was also named after another canal campaigner, John Donnelly who had recently passed away. Along with a small band of enthusiasts they had rallied public opinion against such proposals as filling in the city section for a car park. With many other commitments to attend to,

Rowan soon passed the leadership of the branch to local historian and sailor Sean Patterson, who had already done a lot to highlight the potential of the Ship Canal. In 1998 Sean had been instrumental in bringing the Asgard to Newry and later the Balmoral and the Ocean Youth Club tall ships. Due to his wife's illness Sean resigned in 2007 and Oliver McGauley took over the role as Chairman.

Hunt assembles at Knockbridge on the Newry Canal

Newry Canal Lighters moored at Newry (above) and Portadown (below)

Oliver was another veteran of the Preservation Society and a keen angler who had worked hard to confirm the Ship Canal as an important fishing venue. The world angling championships were held on the canal in 1980. In 2010, Peter Maxwell who with Geraldine Foley had recently returned from a solo round the world boat trip took over as chairman and secretary respectively.

The Newry Canal is really a waterway in two parts. The Ship Canal joins Newry city to Carlingford Lough and has always remained operational, but since the port closed to commercial traffic in 1974 there seemed to be a lack of vision for how best to develop both it and the canal basin. From its inception, the branch encouraged local yachts to visit and demonstrated the potential for a marina in the Albert Basin. There was quite a struggle to get the local council to accept that visiting yachts weren't simply a nuisance but an asset to the city of Newry and the surrounding area. The basin is now a popular winter berth for local yachts, there

Participants in the Newry Canal small boats Rally 2010

One of the first public events held by the branch was a walk to celebrate the completion of the final restored towpath stage in November 2005. Now some 250,000 visits per year are made to the towpath and the branch targets these visitors to gather support for eventual restoration.

Lobbying for restoration may be a worthy activity but it's hardly enough to keep a branch alive and growing. At one stage membership declined to a handful of attendees at monthly meetings with a very slim agenda. Branch officers decided to start a work party programme to inject new enthusiasm into the branch. It took three years to get permission from the local councils to work on the canal, and another three to build up a relationship of trust with the various government agencies that have responsibility for the drainage and heritage aspects of the canal. It has, however, been worth the effort and the branch is now a committed and effective group of active volunteers with a wide range of activities from eradicating invasive species to creating an interactive heritage map for use with mobile phones. In 2011 we began a project to re-open a short section of canal close to Newry with two locks which had their gates reinstated in 1998 but had since fallen into dereliction. By the autumn of 2014 we should be in a position to have a small boat rally from Sand's Mill on the edge of Newry City Centre up through the two locks to St Colman's College 1.5 miles away. This will be the first traffic on this section of the canal in more than half a century.

were seventeen in 2012, and this variety of boats lends colour and life to the now vibrant quayside. Without the IWAI Newry Branch, this certainly would not have happened; the then branch secretary Paul Hoben was like a terrier with a bone and tirelessly pursued the Council until he achieved success.

The inland canal was completed in 1741 and is the oldest summit canal in these islands running 18 miles between Newry and Portadown. The line of the canal is intact and is a designated watercourse with an important drainage role. It is owned by the four local councils that border it and there were numerous efforts in the late 1990s to source funding for complete restoration. All efforts to re-open the waterway were unsuccessful but the towpath had been restored largely funded by Sustrans, an organisation which promotes cycling. It has proved extremely attractive as an off-road cycle route as well as a long distance walk.

North Barrow Branch

Kathleen Cross

The Lovely Barrow

The North Barrow Branch was formed in the late 1990's, as a group of us were concerned that the River Barrow and the Grand Canal flowing through our town, Athy was not being used. We got together and put our thinking hats on to see how we could showcase our waterway so the North Barrow Branch was born. We cover from Rathangan in County Kildare to Milford in County Carlow.

The founding committee were Tom Yates, Chairperson; James Reeves, Secretary; Michael Rowan, Treasurer; committee members were John Lynch, Dave Henshaw, the late Pat Henshaw and Kathleen Cross. We organised a boat rally with over thirty boats from all over taking part and continued the rallies for the next few years. Unfortunately rallies stopped and all was quiet on the river again. However three years ago we decided to have a water festival; this was a great success and we have done so since with another one planned for next May.

From the beginning of the North Barrow branch we started doing a clean up on the river and canal banks which we have continued over the years. We can now boast of a floating jetty on the River Barrow in the town centre and free mooring is available for long or short-term mooring. All will be very welcome, if only to do some shopping to stock up on provisions, or visit our heritage centre, view Whites Castle, visit our unique Dominican Church, all within minutes of our mooring point.

On a finishing note we are the proud winners of the Barrow awards for 2013.

Offaly Branch

John Dolan

The Offaly Branch of the Inland Waterways Association was formed on the 4th of December 1972, a milestone that was reported in the March 1973 edition of Inland Waterways News. Its remit covered Edenderry, Daingean, Ferbane and Shannon Harbour, along with Tullamore.

Its founding officers were John V. McNamara, Chairman; Michael Thomas, Vice-Chairman; Tom Farrell, Hon Secretary and S Egan, Hon Treasurer.

Along with the officers, founder members included, Eugene McMenamin, P V.Egan, Frank Egan

107B Grand Canal barge restored by the Offaly branch at the Fleadh (above) and moored at Ballycommon on the Grand Canal

(Birr), Harry Egan, Brian Mahon, Ciaran Costello, Tom Coughlan, Michael Murphy, Ollie Toner, Ned Davis, Seamus Mahon and Brian Adams. Mrs Ruth Heard, IWAI National President, attended the inaugural meeting at which time there were in excess of ten paid up members. P.V.Egan, John McNamara and Mike Thomas also served on the national council of IWAI.

Independent 7 December 1963. It outlined that a large protest was organised in Tullamore against the proposed closure of 5 1/2 miles of the Grand Canal in Dublin for sewerage purpose by Dublin Corporation. The paper advises that the meeting, which filled the ballroom of Hayes Hotel, was sponsored by Tullamore branch of the Inland Waterway Association and Mr F. J. Egan (junior) chairman of the branch presided.

Some of the issues which brought about the founding of the Offaly branch in 1972 were to do with developing the canal in Tullamore as an attractive amenity, by improving the footpaths, railings, seating etc. and planting trees on the banks. The association also requested that a boat slip be provided in the harbour and a lifting bridge to improve access, both of these goals were in fact achieved by the mid 1970's.

The Offaly Branch ran a very successful Rally for 11 years together with the Boatman's Ball in the Bridge House, from the mid '70s to the mid '80s. Since 1972, the Branch has had a number of different Chairpersons including John V. McNamara who was Chair in 1972; Jim Ridgeway served from 1990 to 2000; Tim Meehan from 2000 to 2007 and Bernadette Quinn from 2007 to 2010 when John Dolan took over and is the current chair.

The Branch has been extremely active on many fronts over the years in areas including education, historical and leisure related events. The very successful "Know your boat" courses have been

In researching for this publication the Branch have uncovered references in a number of papers to a Tullamore Branch of the IWAI in the 1960's, with particular reference to the Midlands protest against Canal closures noted in the Offaly

Fleadh in TullamoreH

The Offaly Branch in recent years have enjoyed success with three Float to the Fleadh events 2007 to 2009, the Boat to the Banjo Festival in 2012 and the Offaly Floating Festival and Gathering event in 2013, which included a 2 day Youth workshop with St Marys Youth and Community Centre and the production of the young persons' work in a 2014 Calendar. Forty years later we now have a vibrant branch with 57 Members. Our current Officers are John Dolan, Chairman; Alan Hughes, Hon Secretary (both on national council); Rosemary Colton, Hon Treasurer; Bernadette Quinn, Vice chair/ PRO; Ronnie Colton Webmaster and Charlie Kelleher (Membership Secretary).

Powerboat Branch

Paul Garland

The Branch was formed in Cox's Bar, Dromod on the 21st. January 2011; there were twenty-two people in the room and as soon as Paul Garland who was the current President started the proceedings, there were protests from some local residents who refused to identify themselves, but were happy to speak on behalf of the village of Dromod saying that we were not welcome; they obviously perceived us a threat to the peace and quiet of Dromod! Efforts were made to explain the ethos of the Association and the very reason for the Branch was to promote the responsible use of Powerboats; after some discussion they left.

run by the Branch in association with Athlone Institute of Technology for the past 10 years; the Branch is a supporter of the 107 B Project. This barge is used as a floating exhibition and educational space travelling the Waterway's system, promoting the heritage of the Grand Canal.

Launch of the powerboat branch

Cormac Smith was elected as the Chairman, Hugo Green as the Hon Treasurer and Paul Garland as Hon Secretary. An inaugural Branch Meeting was arranged to structure and put together a programme of events for the incoming year.

Like all Branches and probably the Association itself, a lot of work behind the scenes had taken place before the Branch was launched. I had seen some opportunities through my training with the Irish Sailing Association that there was a change in the way some people were using their boats and indeed the boats themselves were of a different variety. During the early two thousands, sports boats and rigid inflatable boats (RIB's) were gaining popularity, both with trailer boaters and holiday home owners. The majority of boaters were normal families who just wanted to get out on the water. The inland waterways system, with the ease

of launching, abundance of jetties, lack of tides, and fresh water proved very attractive cruising grounds. Cormac Smith approached me in late 2010 looking for the Association's assistance in bringing the UK Classic Motorboat Association to the Shannon. It was an opportunity not to be missed, his enthusiasm, coupled with the willingness of the IWAI, made all the stars align and very quickly led to the formation of The Powerboat Branch.

A really well run Classic Powerboat event in Dromod and Athlone over two Spring Weekends in 2011 put the branch firmly on the map. By promoting dual membership many existing IWAI members were joining and enjoying the events which cover all of Ireland. In the initial few months various letters to the local papers complained about the idea of IWAI promoting power boating, all were responded to and as the branch grew, people saw the benefits of a well structured, well organised branch where people are encouraged to use their boats responsibly and have fun.

The branch is now three years old and while still very much a baby branch, we have our voice and are well organized with a dozen events a year, membership heading for fifty and another hundred followers on FaceBook! We have no fixed cruising area, we sail the rivers and occasionally off the coast of Ireland even in the winter months as there are so many other IWAI events during the summer for us to join. As we continue to expand the branch, through fun and learning we feel

In the Grand Canal Basin in Dublin

that it can be a primary branch for those interested, or to add another dimension to the cruiser/barge people who may want to get more out of a RIB or sports boat. All the activities of the IWAI rely on voluntary members thinking like-minded thoughts and converting them into events but in many cases the unsung heroes of the Association are wives/husbands and partners quietly oiling the process; they know who they are, but I just hope they realise how much they are appreciated.

River Bann and Lough Neagh Association Branch

Alaistair Uprichard and Lord Raymond O'Neill.

"We are not a Conservation Society; we are not a Navigation Society. We do not necessarily agree with any Government or Local Government in-terest, nor do we have any other specialised interest. We exist for the benefit of the River Bann and Lough Neagh and hope to extend our influence over associated waters"; the raison d'etre of RBLNA, as defined by its Founding Father, Eric Seaton.

Eric and a few friends initiated the River Bann Boat Club, the fore-runner of RBLNA on 20th Feb. 1962 at his home, Drumslade, north of Coleraine, later to develop as Seaton's Marina. It was initially a speed-boat Club but soon accepted dinghies and eventually cruisers. The Clubhouse was a WW2 motor launch referred to as ML, which by constant use became 'Emily'. In 1967 there was talk of closing the Lower Bann as a navigable waterway. A public meeting was held in Coleraine Town Hall at which a steering com-

Welcome to the lower Bann – lock at Toome

Boat Rally on lower Bann

particularly remember a large event at Portglenone when a helicopter gave air/sea rescue displays; a concours d'elegance was usually a feature of these events as well.

When the Lough Neagh Development Association collapsed and was merged with the River Bann Association, the responsibilities of the organisation expanded considerably. Nevertheless, membership was never very large but we did manage to keep the problems in the public mind and influence Government in various ways. At a later stage, the Lough Neagh and River Bann Advisory Committees came into being. These were both Government sponsored and therefore the problems were kept in the public eye. Sadly, lack of finance has meant that these have faded away. But we still have the Lough Neagh Partnership which is sponsored by the Local Authorities, with assistance from various grant-aiding bodies.

mittee was formed under the patronage of Lord O'Neill. The RBBC became The River Bann and Lough Neagh Association. Forty-seven years later Lord O'Neill is still the Patron and is still very much involved in Branch activities. In the early years the organisation was principally aimed at saving and maintaining the Upper Bann navigation, the committee always tried to involve members who were interested in the wildlife and fishing aspects of the area, although I think we were only relatively successful in recruiting members with relevant expertise, and there was always a bias towards boating.

In the early years meetings took place in the Leighinmohr House Hotel and the Wild Duck Inn at Portglenone. Because of the need to encourage use of the river as much as possible, several rallies took place at key points on the system. I

The original membership contained many well-known and influential personalities and they got things done! While reading the minutes of those early meetings it became obvious that the group had a 'finger in every pie', which in general eliminated the lengthy negotiations so characteristic of modern bureaucracy. Signage was maintained and extended, regular dredging took place, shallows were removed and locks maintained. A code of conduct for river users was produced and accepted by the local Councils. All this was achieved in an average FOUR meetings per year usually held in the Deerpark Hotel, Antrim.

Up until the formation of the Newry and Portadown Branch of IWAI, the RBLNA 'looked after' the Newry Canal and were instrumental in retaining Moneypenny's Lock and developing it as a Visitor and Canoe Centre, the Blackwater also came under our influence by making easy access available through the dredging of the Maghery Cut.

Thirty years later many of the original members had passed on or left and membership became critically low. This was a major factor in deciding to join IWAI. It was a decision not taken lightly and attracted considerable opposition from a sizeable minority, but in 2001 we became the sixteenth branch of IWAI. The first benefit was the adoption of Lower Bann by Waterways Ireland who does a marvellous job of maintaining the waterway.

RBLNA has the usual round of social activities (dinners, boat rallies, visits, talks, etc) but is unique throughout IWAI in having the Ram's Island Project. In 2003 Lord O'Neill leased Ram's Island to RBLNA to develop as a Wildlife Sanctuary and Visitor Attraction. Under the guidance of Michael Savage and substantial grants from Government Agencies and Antrim Council, groups of volunteers have transformed the island from an inaccessible wilderness to a top-class venue for a day out or even an overnight camp! From 2007 when the majority of the initial work was completed visitor numbers have averaged 8,000 per year!

Since 1967 Government quangos, Council Committees and Local Initiatives have appeared regularly and just as regularly disappeared without trace. Over the 47 years of its existence RBLNA has been consistent in maintaining the integrity set out by Eric Seaton and its advice is much respected in all quarters. As our current Chairman told a Stormont Committee, "Ignore us at your peril!"

Shannon Harbour Branch

Ruth Heard

Ruins of the old hotel at Shannon Harbour

The first Shannon Harbour Boat Rally was held in 1971 organised by a group of people who kept their boats there and was aimed specifically at owners who had ex-canal boats. John Weaving always objected to the use of the term "barge" hence the use of "Canal Boat" in the name of the rally.

In 1972 an Offaly Branch of the IWAI was established and Shannon Harbour came within the area covered by it but the rally continued to be organised by a committee independent of the IWAI. By the 1980's the number of boats using Shannon Harbour on a regular basis had increased and a group of boat owners decided to form an IWAI branch to carry out improvement works and the rally committee agreed to a merger. The rally continues to be held annually on the weekend closest to the summer solstice in June and in addition to canal boats, all types of boats are welcomed.

The Slaney Estary

Slaney Branch
Catherine Malone

The late Cecil G Miller, a keen boater and inland waterways enthusiast, compiled the *Slaney Guide* to the tidal section of the river from Wexford Harbour to Enniscorthy, which was published in 1987. His main aim in producing the Guide was to encourage others to use and enjoy the river, as he was doing.

The idea of a Slaney Branch was cooked up between Cecil and his good friend David Killeen, while they were on a Shannon Rally in 1988. They organised an informal meeting in the Wexford Harbour Boat and Tennis Club (WHBTC) on 27 January 1989, with a panel of invited guests, which included the then Chairman of the Boat Club, Tom Hore, who said the Club was de-

lighted at the idea that boats would be using the stretch of the water to the 'left' as opposed to heading 'right' out to sea. Cecil outlined the advantages of the inland waterways of Ireland, particularly the Shannon, Barrow, Grand Canal, etc. Arthur Kepple of the Barrow Branch pointed out the advantages of having a 'Branch' and the opportunity to explore the navigable stretches of local rivers and canals in company with other members. Following very enthusiastic discussion, a formal proposal to form the Slaney Branch of the IWAI was proposed by Jim Maguire, seconded by Bill Lett and unanimously approved by all those present. The first Officers of the Branch were then elected:
President: Cecil Miller
Chairman: David Killeen
Secretary: Peter Miller
Treasurer: Jim Maguire
PRO: Michael Poole

The first formal meeting of the Slaney Branch was held on 24 February 1989 in WHBTC. It was decided that the Membership Fee should be £10 Family and £8 Single.

Sadly Cecil passed away in October 1989, but left the legacy of a Branch that has survived to the present day.

The first AGM of the Branch was held on 3 April 1990 and David, Jim and Michael were all re-elected. The late Cecil Dier took on the job of Secretary, a post he held for six years.

The first 'Rally' from Wexford to Enniscorthy took place over the week-end 30 June/1 July 1990, with 16 boats of all shapes and sizes participating. A perpetual trophy, in memory of Cecil, was provided by the Branch to be awarded to the participants scoring the highest marks for boatmanship, safety, etc and also answering the Maguire 'Killer' Quiz, which Jim has continued to compile and tease members on rallies to the present day.

David Killeen continued as Chairman of the Branch, until he took on the mantle of President in 2001. He is as active and enthusiastic now as he was in 1989, and, with his wife Eleanor, has been the Branch representative at Council Meetings.

The late Paddy Hatton took on the role of Secretary from Cecil Dier and continued in this post for ten years until he took on the post of Chairman. He did a fantastic job of keeping the Branch active during his term of office and was greatly missed when he passed away in 2007.

David handed over his Chairmanship to Phillip Scallan, followed by Paddy Hatton, Peter Hussey, Tommy Duggan and Fred Crampton.

In Memory of the late Cecil and Paddy, the Branch installed a 'seat' at Killurin Pier, on the Slaney, a favourite stopping place on rallies for people to relax and enjoy the peace and beauty of the River.

The Branch went from strength to strength for many years, achieving over 40 members at one stage. Sylvester O'Brien introduced a Young Mariners Award, which was a great success for several years while we had junior members. However, as with all organisations, members move on, children grow up and numbers drop, but there is always the challenge to survive!

There have been many enjoyable rallies on the Slaney and on the Barrow in company with the Barrow Branch; dinghy rallies to other rivers and canals in surrounding Counties, and coastal walks. We have had very interesting presentations on a wide variety of topics by Branch Members, Council Members, including the National President of IWAI and other invited guests.

The Slaney Branch is indebted to the Management and Staff of Wexford Harbour Boat and Tennis

Club for the use of their premises for Meetings, Social Functions and the slipway at rally time and also to their Members for supporting IWAI events.

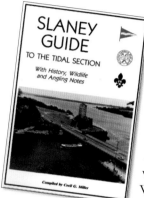

To finish where we started – with the *Slaney Guide* – over the years there have been changes to the navigable channels due to tidal conditions, flooding, etc, particularly in the area of The Patches. The Branch has undertaken a project, with the permission of the Wexford Harbour Master, to survey the area and replace markers to ensure continued safe navigation from Wexford to Enniscorthy and encourage as many boaters as possible to continue using the river, as was the ambition of the late Cecil Miller and all the founding members of the Slaney Branch of the Inland Waterways Association of Ireland

Scarva

Scarva Basin

The Scarva Branch was formed in September 1978. In 1980 the Branch mounted a campaign to restore the Newry Canal while in 1981 a comprehensive Canal Survey was commissioned by Rivers Agency, a department of the government. On 26th September 1987 the Scarva Branch and the Newry Canal Preservation Society organised a boat rally along the ship canal to Victoria Lock. The branch was still very much functioning in 1990 as they welcomed the publication of the Feasibility Study into the re opening of the Newry Canal.

From then records cease and shortly afterwards the lone survivor of the branch, Denis McCartney died in 1991. The N I Branch made numerous appeals to support the Joint Council Canal Committee millennium bid to have the canal reopened and were bitterly disappointed when the bid failed. In 2001 the Northern Ireland Branch, who continued to monitor developments on the canal, wrote letters protesting at the construction of the low level bridge behind the newly opened Scarva visitors centre when it was claimed this sent out the wrong message to the public at large as this was really blocking the navigation. Although those in authority claimed this was only a temporary structure it is interesting to note, it is still in existence today some thirteen years later!

In 2003 the Northern Ireland Branch supported and welcomed efforts to re-open a section at the summit of the Newry Canal. In March 2005 the then President, Brian Cassells in conjunction with Hugh King who was then living locally, formed the Newry Branch, this was the fifth of the new Northern Ireland Branches behind the Erne, RBLNA, Coalisland and Lagan Branches. There were branches in Ballinamore, Tullamore and Mullingar, regretfully documentation regarding these branches is scant.

2012 Royal Canal Rally moored in Mullingar

Mullingar Branch

Ian Bath

The Mullingar Branch of the IWAI was founded in April 1973 and remained in existence into the 1980s but not, if I recall correctly, beyond this time. The first Hon. Secretary was a Miss Dolan, soon to be succeeded by Charles Nolan. The Chairman was Hubert Magee. In the early days meetings were held at least once a month and contacts made with many public figures in Westmeath concerning the condition and future of the Royal Canal. Eventually, in May of the following year, a joint meeting was held with CIE and Westmeath County Council but I was informed that the branch came up against a "stone wall", with very little information being given away.

Following the setting-up by the Dublin Branch of its Royal Canal sub-Committee in February 1974, contact was made with the Mullingar Branch and an invitation was extended to us to join a pre-arranged tour of the canal in the Mullingar area due to take place on 30th June 1974, and to be followed by a meeting held in the Lake County Hotel. There then followed a number of jointly organised events including a public meeting and film show in November, to which Athlone Branch members were also invited.

The close cooperation between the branches continued for some years with, in particular, the holding of the first summit level small boat rally over the weekend of the 17th/18th May 1980. I have no record of any further formal contact with the Mullingar Branch after this date and assume it was later dissolved. However, a branch of the Royal Canal Amenity Group was established in Mullingar in 1985 and has continued the good work.

The Northern Ireland Branch.

Brian Cassells

In 1992 Lough Erne Branch changed its name to the Northern Ireland Branch to assist in canal restoration projects in Northern Ireland. Alan Giff and Jim Wilson, were the officers in charge at that time and Alan was very conscious that there was no branch looking after the interests of the other abandoned navigations, the Ulster, the Lagan, the

Lower Bann, and the Newry/Coalisland canals; thus he changed the name of the Lough Erne Branch to the Northern Ireland Branch. This gave the Branch more status or should I say 'clout' when lobbying politicians and generally keeping a watching brief on any incursion on those waterways. This was the time that the announcement had been made to re-open the old Ballinamore Ballyconnell canal now known as the Shannon Erne Waterway and the branch had been very active in lobbying the Northern politicians even though that was in the period of Direct Rule from Westminister.

Brian Cassells followed Alan in this role and there was regular contact with Rivers Agency and then when it was established, the Department of Culture Arts and Leisure and Waterways Ireland. Over the years there was many a 'run in' with officialdom especially regarding proposed developments on the Newry Canal around Scarva! When River Bann and Lough Neagh Association became a branch of IWAI Victor Hamill, the then Chair of RBLNA rightfully made representation to insure the branch reverted to its original name, indeed it was not long after until the other three Northern Ireland Branches were formed.

The Argory on the Blackwater, Ulster's forgotten river

The Boyne Canal

Not quite the oldest, the Boyne navigation is nevertheless, one of the early attempts to canalise a river. Work commenced in 1748 at the Drogheda end of the waterway where the plan was to link the estuary with Navan though this wasn't achieved until 1800. This waterway initially used sections of the River Boyne with short sections of canal to bypass obstructions. An unusual feature of the early navigation was the need for the horse and barge to switch banks; this was achieved by persuading the horse to mount the barge and then the barge men poling the boat to the opposite bank.

The valley is initially deep sided, forested and very scenic and passes some of the most important early historical sites in Ireland, that of Newgrange, Dowth and Knowth while also skirting the site of the Battle of the Boyne and the new visitor centre. Abandoned since the 1920's it was the dream of members of the Dublin Branch to re-open the waterway, a daunting task by any stretch of the imagination, especially for a voluntary group. Partnered with An Taisce, sometimes referred to as The National Trust for Ireland, this organization is dedicated to preserving Ireland's heritage,

work commenced in 2004. While never really a commercial success, the Boyne Navigation served as a highway to open up the fertile plains of Meath making their produce available to larger centres of population. Coal was delivered to the grain and flower mills especially at Slane and also delivered their produce to the port of Drogheda.

The volunteers began clearing the section beyond the sea lock at Oldbridge of fallen trees and removing debris as the canal had all too often been used as a receptacle for unwanted items. This re-opened stretch would allow navigation for small craft as far as the guard locks constructed to control flooding from this tidal section, indeed the group were quick to organize small boat rallies which attracted interest from all over the country and quickly had the wider membership enthused about this exciting project. The next challenge was the re-instatement of the sea lock and what a test that proved to be. First task was the removal of cased concrete walls, and then with the same enthusiasm as the founder members had shown, new lock gates were made and fitted.

Arguably the next phase of the project is the most exciting of all, the section that will open the navigation as far as the prehistoric sites afore mentioned, at the moment the towpath goes under the footbridge where visitors leave the Bru na Boinne centre to board the buses for Newgrange. Seeing what the folk have achieved to date is impressive. The challenge of repairing the next lock, fitting new gates and repairing the walls will I'm sure prove a doddle, time will tell; watch this space.

Myles Brady & Brian Cassells

Boyne Canal

The navigable River Boyne

139

Sunrise over the inner lakes

Dunrovin Remembered

Ruth Heard

In August 1952 Rory O'Hanlon decided to bring his Dragon yacht, "Firedrake" to the Shannon not only because of the attraction of making a trip on the river but with the ulterior motive of asking to have as many of the opening bridges opened to allow his masted boat through. This was because in that year an Inquiry had been held in Athlone which decided that the existing opening bridge in Athlone, which needed replacing, would have a fixed span and the implications of this for much lower headroom bridges on the river was a cause of concern. With the boat, together with a large bell tent and accompanied by cars and crew, who came and went, the expedition eventually passed through the Grand Canal with the mast following on a canal boat and we headed upstream, eventually arriving at Dunrovin where the bell tent was pitched and I met Harry Rice for the first time. The log records we "dined heavily we sat up until the small hours discussing our cruise with him and drawing on the great fund of local knowledge". We subsequently had many adventures, achieving the objective of getting many of the bridges opened but unfortunately succeeded in damaging the boat when passing through the LoughTap railway bridge by catching the mast in overhead telephone wires. I was to marry Vincent Delany, who had also been a part of the 1952 expedition,

Dunrovin

in the following April 1953 and these were to become critical years for the inland waterways which necessitated frequent visits by us to Dunrovin to devise plans for a way forward. Cynthia, Harry's wife and I used to retire to the kitchen and make tea and smile to each other as Harry and Vincent talked. Much of the time we smiled to each other because they each talked away hardly listening to each other. They both had very definite ideas and they did not always agree with each other. They did not seek our input other than providing tea at regular intervals, as good wives should.

Harry and Vincent were both to die in 1964 before the fruits of all their efforts became clear and they would be quite astonished at how well things have turned out today. Cynthia and I both found ourselves continuing their work. Although Cynthia moved to Kilkenny and let Dunrovin she kept the little room behind the house and frequently returned spending time with the Furlongs next door and becoming a very active member of the Athlone Branch of the IWAI. I found myself occupied with finishing the book Vincent had been working on for David & Charles on the Irish waterways and one thing seemed to lead to another. A few years later I had married Douglas Heard who enjoyed going around filming various waterway events and holidaying on the Shannon. Cynthia and I kept in touch and our paths crossed occasionally and we would laugh as we recalled those sessions in Dunrovin with the raised voices in the next room of those two totally dedicated people.

The Lovely Barrow

R.A.Keppel.

My first voyage down the Barrow was in 1963, in a small eighteen foot boat with a quarter deck. The boat, named "The Dawn", was one which I built myself and was powered by a 25 H.P. Chrysler outboard. This boat served well for many years. The Barrow at that time was in a state of disrepair, overgrown with trees, weeds form the river bed and the bank and the lock gates were almost inoperable. I sheared eight shear pins on the engine between Goresbridge and Graiguenamanagh.

Canoeing on the Barrow

My crew for many of my trips were two other men, one a guitar player and the other a "chef". (Three Men and a Boat!) Having arrived at our destination we moored the boat, and I erected the tent, while the cook prepared a meal and the musician serenaded us. This trip was repeated annually, on the June weekend for many years. The scenery, the peace and the tranquillity of the river Barrow are both very relaxing and refreshing. The joy of boating on the Barrow waters will live with me forever.

The year 1983 saw more changes for me when I launched "Crescendo" having spent 10 months building the boat. This time a 23ft Glen Marine design with a 55 H.P Outboard. The midnight oil was burned on many occasions to achieve my goal, and the boat was launched in Bagenalstown August 1983. Holidaying on the Barrow was even more enjoyable now, not having the trouble of erecting a tent.

St. Mullins with the typical 'Omer' lock house in the background

However not being content with my achievement a few years later I extended the boat by 7 feet and installed a Perkins 4108 engine. This gave me even more comfort with centre cockpit and fore and aft cabins and increased the pleasure of boating on our waterways, particularly the Barrow, Nore and Suir. Then in 1990 I acquired a twin engine Seamaster Commodore which required complete restoration, this took 7 years and is now my pride and joy.

My years on the Barrow were always pleasurable meeting so many people and exchanging experiences and views. One day going downstream I encountered four German people on a hire boat, they were experiencing many problems as the draft of the boat was not suited to the Barrow. I succeeded in getting them to Goresbridge. They moored up for the night; I brought them to a pub in the town where ceili music and craic were in

full swing. The next day I brought them on my boat to St. Mullins and we returned by taxi. A few days later they contacted me and arranged for my wife and myself to join them for dinner. We kept in contact for many years afterwards.

There was another occasion when I was asked by a crew from England if it would be possible for them to navigate the Barrow. I travelled down to St. Mullins, met them and escorted them to Graiguenamanagh on their fifty foot yacht, with all masts down, centreboard up. I said you may encounter delays due to weeds. They questioned me, delays a couple of hours, what is that when you're on a six months cruise! They travelled all the way to the Shannon, up the West Coast of Ireland explored the islands and returned to England. I received a full report and photographs of the trip later. If I were to relate the number of times I had the pleasure of assisting people boating, canoeing and generally enjoying the many recreational facilities provided by the Barrow it would take a whole book.

The Barrow, being the second longest river in Ireland, is navigable for pleasure craft from Athy to St.Mullins, this being made possible by the weirs and lateral canals. Dick Warner once said it was no river for amateurs with "Flash floods and unprotected weirs" yet in my fifty years boating I have never witnessed anyone experiencing difficulties with the aforementioned, yes there may be some difficulties with draft during a dry summer and especially since water extraction in Athy commenced, midsummer 2013. Talking to some of the Heritage boat people recently they said "The Shannon is lovely but the Barrow is Heaven".

I am privileged and honoured to be a judge of the Barrow Awards Scheme. This is a scheme started about thirty two years ago by Pat Nolan of South East Rural Tourism where towns along the river are encouraged to improve the facilities and appearance of their villages. This work keeps me in regular contact with all of the people along the beautiful Barrow river valley.

Some few years ago I was asked by Sean Rock, R.T.E. presenter, to set up interviews with people who live along the river Barrow. We started in the Slieve Bloom Mountains where the Barrow rises, visited every village and town interviewing people along the way and finishing up at Cheek Point where the river reaches the estuary. The recording was later presented by Sean on a radio programme.

My ramblings could go on forever, interviews with Michael Ryan for Nationwide and many others. My words of encouragement would be, "Visit the Barrow by water or otherwise and experience the beauty and tranquillity of the most enchanting river in Ireland."

Nautical Nostalgia
By Dick Warner

Dick Warner

My total immersion in the world of the inland waterways began in the mid 1970s. Before that, for as long as I can remember, I'd been fascinated by water, fishing and small boats. But my first big boat, by which I mean one big enough to sleep on in reasonable comfort, arrived as the result of a personal housing crisis and I began my cruising life as a live-aboard.

"Naida" was an elderly 32-foot wooden cruiser, which the broker, of course, described as a gentleman's motor yacht. She was lying in Garrykennedy and the trip back to Hazelhatch, where I'd decided to do my living aboard, was both eventful and educational. Many of the events were caused by a highly temperamental hydraulic linkage to the gearbox which, nine times out of ten, refused to select neutral. The fact that she was elderly was attested to by a brass builder's plate on a bulkhead and, somewhat hypnotised by it, I decided to take her back to her birthplace on the Clyde to celebrate her fiftieth birthday. The passage from Hazelhatch to the Clyde and on through the Inner Hebrides and western Scotland was even more eventful and educational and when I finally got back, safe and sound, to the Grand Canal I decided to limit myself to more modest cruising grounds. I explored southwards to the Barrow and westwards to the Shannon.

This has continued for forty years, in various different boats, and I hope it will continue for a few more. A lot of things have changed over that period of time. In fact there have been four changes of administration --- CIE, the OPW, Duchas and Waterways Ireland. The Shannon, and latterly the Shannon/Erne, have changed from being dominated by hire boats, with a small number of private owners, who were mostly very enthusiastic, highly skilled and often in quite modest craft. Then came the tiger years, the hire fleets began their decline, the private boats got bigger but their skippers and crews often lacked the skills and the manners of the earlier breed. Now there is another change in progress and the processes of waterways evolution seem to be assuring the survival of the fittest.

The canals and the Barrow Navigation have changed as well. The re-opening of the Royal is obviously of huge significance and we should probably be patient with some of its teething troubles. The Grand and the Barrow are not perfect but I've never seen them in better condition. It's easy to forget what it was like when there were no jetties at locks on the Grand and when a trip on the Barrow in summer meant the boat running aground on a regular basis. But some good things

have been lost. The Grand was always a nursery for boaters, usually boaters with very little money. They bought hulks cheaply, worked very hard on them and slowly climbed the ladder towards cruising comfort. There was a huge sense of community and a great deal of mutual help. I've enjoyed the company of so many of these people over the years but it seems to me they're declining in numbers.

The better standards of maintenance and the increase in boating amenities along our waterways have come with a price tag. In the case of the new Bye-laws that are proposed as I write this, it's a literal price tag. Our canal systems are just becoming too expensive for many people. There's also a metaphorical price tag. The easy-going freedom that was a major attraction of our waterways is being eroded by an attitude of increasingly regimental regulation.

The Shannon has escaped much of this because the Shannon has always been a successful public/private partnership. Private enterprise along the rest of our waterways has dwindled until Lowtown Marine, where I keep my current boat, has become its last embattled outpost. The state has won almost total control and is displaying some of the less attractive aspects of state control --- over-regulation, over-taxation and a refusal to listen.

I look back at forty years on our waterways with great gratitude for the pleasure they have given me. I look forward with some nervousness.

Early Days On The Shannon

By Sam Herraghty

Clonmacnoise – Heritage abounds on the Shannon

"As it was in the Beginning"

The beginning for me was the 1940s; I was born in an area of Athlone called the Strand. The Strand conjures up visions of beautiful beaches and the sea, not so, the Strand was a working area. There were three boat builders with premises along the water front, Thomas Norton was where the funeral home is today, Charley Ward was next to him, he lived in the last house on the block, next to the Friary and the whole car park was his boat yard then. The Brown brothers, Teddy and Frankie built their boats further up, closer to the bridge.

There was an Eel Fishery there too, a big black monstrosity, built from concrete and galvanised sheeting. The bottom half of the building was a huge tank for holding eels, with vertical steel bars at each end of the tank close enough to stop eels from escaping while letting the river run through. The upper level of the building housed all the equipment used by the fishermen, but it also had living accommodation where the men would stay the nights the eels were on the run. As anyone who ever set a night line would tell you, you have to be up before the eels, at the break of day or they'll be gone. In later years the eel shed as it was called locally was used by the Fishery Bailiffs to store confiscated engines and equipment taken from fishermen who were deemed to be poaching. The story goes, that some of these poaching gentlemen reconfiscated their engines and equipment and in doing so set the whole place ablaze, by accident of course. Many a good dinner I had of eels and rashers back then and even though fishing for eels is currently banned if one should jump into my boat I'd have to think long and hard before I'd throw him back into the river.

Further up from the eel shed there was a coal yard, where the coal was delivered to Athlone by barge. I don't remember much about that but I do remember when they closed the coal yard and built the sweet factory there, I can still taste those sweets. I suppose I should have started by saying that the Strand is the opposite side of the river from the docks, which was a hive of industry back then. You had the Guinness depot, a CIE depot, Lyster's Saw Mill and below the lock you had the

Clockwise from above: The swing bridge at Athlone:
the sluices: The old starch factory being demolished.

old starch factory, which was once a distillery and later a woollen mill; that's where the apartments stand today. It was a busy place then with the Guinness barges bringing their sacred cargos to Athlone and beyond, and the flour boats bringing their cargos from Odlums in Limerick. Lots of goods travelled up and down the river those times as it was the only highway in the country that didn't have potholes in it!

What fun we had being reared on the river; we were like ducks always either in the water or on the water, swimming, fishing and messing about in boats. The best sport of all was sniggling perch,that was some ceremony. Firstly you need a net to catch perch fry. Where do you get a net, well you make one? You need three jute sacks, split them along the sides and sew the ends of them to each other until you have a long strip of jute; in

the middle of your length of jute you cut a hole in the jute and sew an old pillow case into it to create a pocket. At each end you nailed the jute to a four foot pole; on the top side of your net you put floats and on the bottom you put lead weights. You are now ready to catch the fry; you would set your net with a person on the poles at each end, in shallow water while some of the boys in swim suits would drive the fry towards the net. The net would be closed by bringing the two poles together and winding them around each other thus reducing the circle, the fry would then see the white of the pillow case, think it was an opening and swim into it and bingo you had a pillow case full of perch fry. The next part of the process was to transfer the fry in to containers; these hi-tech containers were Jacob's biscuit tins with a series of small holes around the tops of the tin which allowed fresh water to pass through the container. These containers would hang from the crug or oar peg of the boat while you fished and periodically you would top up a smaller container which you would keep in the boat.

August was the best time for sniggling perch, it would be no problem to bring home four or five dozen lake perch of an evening with maybe three or four people fishing from that boat. When I say 'lake perch' there is a marked difference between river perch and lake perch; the river perch are white on the underside and tend to be smaller, while the lake perch are sort of golden underneath and are bigger, stronger and are better fighters. What would you do with four or five dozen perch when you return home in the evening? No problem, there would be lots of people waiting for the boats to come home with their catch, free fish, remember there was no Dunnes or Tesco back then.

You are going to ask me how do you prepare and cook a nice big perch. First you make an incision each side of the dorsel fin, from the head to the tail then catch the fin near the tail and pull, and the whole thing will come out like a zip. Make a cut each side at the gills, then run your knife between the skin and the flesh; when that's done you can fillet the fish leaving the head attached to the rest of the carcase. Take your fillets, dip them in egg and then into bread crumbs and fry; beautiful.

I should have mentioned that the method of fishing or sniggling with fry was to place a live perch fry onto an eel hook or similar with of course the hook tied to your fishing line. It was then dangled over the side of the boat waiting for the next shoal of perch to pass by. In the event of a shortage of fishing rods a hazel rod with a piece of line tied to the end of it would suffice. But of course fishing with live bait has long been prohibited; I wonder how worms feel about that. During the summers when the weir wall was dry and school was over, we would fish on the lower side of the wall and at the sluices. There was a great perch hole just where the weir wall had breached back in 1934, before my time that is; the resultant flow of the water through the gap created this hole and if you happen to be in Athlone in the summer and the wall is dry you can walk out along it and see where it was repaired with concrete and you can see some of the original cut stones lying below the wall. Lying in my bed at night during the long hot summers we used to get back then, I would listen to the music of the water flowing over the weir and through the sluices, and times when I'd be away from home I would miss it.

Along the Strand the boat builders would hire out row boats during the summer, some were hired by fishermen and others by local people who just

Weigh- in of a pike fishing competition by the Athlone Anglers around the late 50s early

wanted to spend a leisurely evening rowing their wives or girlfriends up the river, I remember the back seats of these boats would have a back rest for the relaxation of the passenger. There were outboard engines at the time Eltos, Anzanis and even a few early Johnson and Evinrude. The problem was you nearly needed to be an engineer to operate one of them; firstly you needed a great big wet battery sitting beside you because the early engines did not have built-in magnetos so the battery provided the spark. There were no pull cords just a handle on top of the flywheel and you had to spin this flywheel in such a way that if the machine back fired you didn't break your thumb or land up in the river behind the boat. They were also very very noisy and expensive, and as money must have just been invented, or so it seemed because there wasn't much of it around, only the well-to-do could afford one.

My father who was a Donegal man, came from a fishing family in Downings and always had a boat, a seventeen foot clinker built row-boat and each Sunday during the fishing season my father Mick, myself and his pal Joe and the rest of the Anglers' Association would take part in pike fishing competitions on Lough Ree. They would start at eleven o'clock in the morning and finish at six in the evening, the only thing was, no-one had an outboard engine. You had to row up to the start at the old boathouse near the white buoy to register and pay your subscription and then row all day, hour on and hour off. Thank God I was too young but as I got older I used to take short turns! There was a pub called the Thatch owned by Paddy Harkens and it was just a few fields down from the Yacht Club and that's where most of the weigh-ins were held, then into the pub for refreshments and a sing song and then row home again. When the British Seagull, that famous outboard, arrived not everyone could afford one, luckily Mick and Joe could; this was great, pull the cord and away you go. Unfortunately as not everyone had an engine, you were only allowed to use your engine to get to the start of a competition and then we rowed all day long while the engine sat on the back of the boat smiling at us, while we fished. It was nice to have the engine when we came out of the Thatch and we even used to tow some of the engineless boats back to town after the sing song. Eventually everyone got engines which levelled the playing field and it was then allowable to use them during the competition opening up much more of the lake to the fishermen.

Well enough of these ramblings about the old days, but I must say that the river Shannon and its lakes have played a big part in my life and that of my family. In the late fifties our family moved to England where work was plentiful and no matter where I worked, be it England, South Africa or the Middle East, when I closed my eyes at night it was the Shannon I saw in my mind's eye. In 1970, I returned to Ireland for a holiday and never went back, bought a row boat and engine, met Sheila, got married and settled down. We added four children to our little family Donie, Niamh, Ruairi and Oona and each time we had an addition we had to get a bigger boat; they say there are four boats in every home, I guess that must be about right. The children had a most wonderful youth, swimming, sailing, fishing and enjoying the great outdoors. The two boys took to the sailing in a big way and were part on the crew of the very successful Chieftain which won the Fastnet and its class in the Sydney to Hobart and many more international races. The two girls stuck to the Shannon and along with Donie are part of the crew of the Lough Ree RNLI life boat.

Having had so much pleasure from the Shannon, both myself and Sheila have tried in our own small way to give something back; we have served on the Kildare Branch, the Athlone Branch, Council, the Shannon Harbour Rally Committee and the Shannon Rally Committee. In fact this year's Shannon Boat Rally will be the thirty-fifth rally the crew of the "Dunross", have entered without missing one. We now have three generations crewing the "Dunross" when we include our grandson Sam. Where did we get the name "Dunross"? Well, just look at the initials of our children and add Sheila and Sam to that! What about the U? Well we had a canary called Ulick but he died! Along with the wonderful people I met along the river, there were also lots of fantastic musicians, most of whom I've had the pleasure to play with; there was Kieran Walsh, the Henshaws, Sean Matthews and Larry Benson just to mention a few; sadly some of them have passed on to the big band in the sky, but they would be glad to see a new generation following along behind them. We must not forget the good times we had, or our responsibility to look after the waterways for the people coming behind us.

Dunrovin

Alison Alderton

I asked Alison Alterton, who recently rented the property, to write me a piece telling of her memories of Dunrovin, her simplistic poetic description for me says it all; surely we can devise a future for something that truly epitomises the philosophy of our Association.

The grounds of Dunrovin are entered through a cast iron gateway set into a hedge which from the roadside is easily missed. The long driveway is overhung by a rich variety of trees and shrubs before turning sharply to plummet down into the darkness of a wood where small birds flit in and out of low-lying branches. Through the leafy shade the shimmering sapphire blue of Lough Ree's inner lakes makes a tantalising appearance, glinting between the alder, beech, birch, spruce and willow trees. Levelling, the driveway enters a small clearing where in all its glory stands Colonel Harry Rice's Nissen hut and birthplace of the IWAI. Its white-washed walls with rambling pink roses and distinctive barrel roof immediately tug at my heart strings, and so begins my love affair with this historical place and the changing seasons which shape it.

Spring: With winter's blanket lifted, clumps of wood anemones and primroses herald the arrival of spring. These give way to blue bells, whose mutant white blooms dominate. As the weather warms there is a sense of anticipation in the air. Blue tits have raised a brood in the bird box made by my father. The morning they fledge I am drawn outside by a commotion to discover the youngsters gingerly balancing on the sweeping branches of a macrocarpa tree, the proud parents busily fussing over them.

Ferns uncoil from between the stone terraces, the large leathery leaves of bergenia send up clusters of bright pink flowers. Aquilegias, known to me since a child as granny's bonnets appear everywhere. As described in Harry Rice's book, *Thanks for the Memory*, they trip and tumble over the rocky outcrops towards the lake creating the appearance of a babbling brook and waterfall. Here and there

Dunrovin

the bright blue and odd white blooms are pierced by yellow petals of Himalayan poppies, like spots of sunshine reflecting on water.

Barge at Dunrovin dock

Summer: Backed by a thousand shades of green, the woodland edge is bordered with purple and white blooms of foxglove spires and frothy clouds

Autumn at Dunrovin

of cow parsley which seem to float weightlessly above the other vegetation. Armadas of airborne insects patrol the water's edge where wild flowers are most abundant. Brambles march tirelessly across the pathways, there is little I can do to stop them but the flowers are attractive and will provide bountiful fruit later in the season. The trees, heavy with leaf, create a pleasant shady coolness to escape the sun's rays and plenty of places to tie the hammock. Swinging in dappled sunlight accompanied by the sound of the lapping lake has become a favourite past time!

The rowing club hold their annual regatta transforming the area into a bustling headquarters with Dunrovin playing host to the open lake boats used by organisers marking out the course. Keen athletes practising for Athlone's Triathlon swim past the peaceful gardens in a wild frenzy from where we have grand stand views. During the balmy days of summer my barge nestles in Dunrovin's dock or when water levels are low she gently bobs on a buoy in the bay whilst craft of all types constantly trundle back and forth. Quigley's marina and Waveline hire base on the opposite shore are a hive of activity, muffled voices carry across the water; it is the sound of summer at Dunrovin.

Autumn: Plopping sounds from the dock at dawn reveal an otter playfully twisting over and over in the shallows, bolder mink are a frequent sight but this is the first time an otter has visited. He doesn't stay long, diving below the surface and heading into deeper water leaving a trail of bubbles. Rain showers drift in distorting the far reaching views bringing a welcome coolness to the air. The distant laughter of children playing at Coosan Point and the throbbing of boat engines on the lake begins to quieten. The garden seems to sigh with relief, it has put on a show all summer and now it can relax. Leaves flutter down creating a crispy carpet of russet and golden hues for me to kick my way through during daily strolls.

A kingfisher perches on the bright red dogwood, his beady eye scanning the water; if I venture outside he quickly flees leaving no more than a flash of metallic turquoise and a shrill mocking cry to shatter the silence. Evenings are spellbinding especially when the moon is bright; it silhouettes the treetops and creates a slinky silver trail stretching out across the lake like an illuminated pathway.

Winter: Thick mists create a strange violet glow to

Winters misty violet glow

the lake which penetrates deep into Dunrovin's grounds. Dampness coats the vegetation in dewy droplets which glisten and glimmer on the spider webs and creates a weighty droop to the wispy wands of the pendulous sedge. As snow falls and the lake freezes quietness descends broken only in the evenings when the temperatures plummet and the refreezing ice sounds as if an orchestra is tuning-up far away across the icy expanse. Smoke from the turf fire often sweeps downwards to the lake before rising to create a pleasant intoxicating veil. Even with the fire roaring it is often chilly in the cottage, ice on the inside of the picture windows is a frequent early morning occurrence.

Moorhens and ducks peck at scraps which the smaller birds have dropped from the bird table whilst flocks of redwings tired from migration seek shelter in the woods. A fox appears silently making his way through the grounds leaving only footprints in the snow beneath which the gardens slumber in preparation for the spring

***

My home for two years, Dunrovin means so much more to me than a house standing in an acre of woodland. Not only does the word conjure up a magical enchanting place but also a unique atmosphere. Anyone privileged to spend time at Dunrovin will realise it is a living and breathing place, the heart, the soul, the very essence of the IWAI and all it stands for.

Barrow Branch in the late 60s and early 70s
by Padraic O Brolchain

On my arrival in Carlow in 1967, I joined the Barrow Branch of the IWAI. My dream was to buy an old canal boat, restore it, and cruise the waterways with my family. I also wanted to join the organisation that was doing so much to make this possible. I met Bill Duggan and Bertie Shirley, the one a solicitor the other a garage owner, mechanic and hire boat operator. Between them they were the Barrow Branch.

They ranged up and down the Barrow with work parties clearing obstructions, putting in markers and haranguing CIE to do what minimum maintenance they could afford. John MacNamara,

CIE's canal engineer, was based in Tullamore and to give him his due he attended our meetings and did his best with what resource he had. Bertie's hire boats were pretty basic but worked most of the time. In one or other of these we would set off on a project, usually decided by Bill. We would take a picnic. Bertie invented and made many ingenious devices. We had a pile driver operated by two people. A clamp was placed around a piece of treated timber and this device fitted over it. In this way we drove in posts to which we attached red and black round and square shapes, to mark the navigation. Bertie also developed a strange device which we used to repair the red and black paint on bridges, while the boat from which we worked was held in position against the current.

One season with an investment in some Cassaron G we succeeded in keeping two still water sections (canal cuts) weed free for the summer to the dual benefit of boaters and fishermen. At our next AGM Bill made hay with poor John MacNamara on this subject. He led him on by asking why CIE had not used it and then sprung the trap when John said that tests would first have to be carried out. Cassaron G was later used on the canals with success, but is no longer considered to be an acceptable method of weed control. Cutting is preferred for ecological reasons.

One Easter we had a jointly organised Rally when members of Dublin Branch brought their boats to Carlow. I first met people like the Heards, the Denhams, the Blakes and many others. This was the beginning of many later friendships. Among the unplanned excitements of the week-end we were treated to a wheelhouse removal by the treacherous Carlow Bridge. We had many clean-ups, Dublin Branch organised a joint clean-up of the cut at Bagenalstown where Dr. Peter Denham's family owned an old mill. That was a hard but enjoyable day of work. A large number of eels were acquired by a few enterprising individuals with the use of forks when the section dried out. The technique used required a party of three, one digger with a fork who whipped the eels from the mud high up the bank, and two catchers to grab the eels and pop them into a sack before they wriggled away.

Cecil Miller with his boat "Calloo" was a regular visitor to events and to our meetings. I am never quite sure as to how much he contributed to the first charts of the Barrow and the Suir, copies of which were given to me by Bill Duggan. Bill certainly had a significant part in this work. This was in the days before the current range of charts were even thought of. These early charts were simple affairs printed on a Roneo machine, a predecessor of the Xerox copier, using wax templates which had a limited life.

Shannon Rally-Early Days

David Killeen

In the early days of the Shannon Rally the fleet tended to undertake marathon voyages. For instance, we started the 1962 Rally from the Lough Ree Yacht Club in Athlone at 7 a.m. and reached our destination, Carrick-on-Shannon, at around 9 p.m. that night. My boat was a 505 sailing dinghy equipped with spinnaker and trapeze, but with no engine. We were lucky to have a fair wind all the way, and while we did use the spinnaker, we did not have to put any of the crew out on the trapeze. The crew was my sister Maeve and a friend, Anne O'Rahilly, who both came from Dublin for the week. I had towed the 505 from Wexford the previous day, driving a Mini Cooper (registration number BMI 505).

Lanesborough Bridge proved to be the first problem solved quickly by a kind rallier who loaned us a row-boat. The 505 floated well on her side with the mast parallel to the water. One of us held her in that position while the others rowed the boat through the bridge. This operation had to be repeated for every bridge and ESB power line the whole way to Carrick!

Another heart-stopping moment occurred on the Jamestown Canal, by that time tiredness had set in but the wind had increased and we were actually planning up the canal. A bridge came into view and the problem was how to stop. We had to get off the plane by turning right around into the wind, and I was not sure it could be done in the narrow canal! However, she turned on the proverbial sixpence and so all was well. At that stage, Maureen Browne took pity on us and towed us the last ten miles into Carrick-on-Shannon.

A feature of the early Rallies was that they were sponsored by Esso, who supplied the whole fleet of some 150 boats with free fuel for the week. Not to be out done, Shell Oil sent a fully loaded oil tanker with strict instruction to the driver to get rid of the fuel regardless! This led to such a demand for five-gallon drums that they could not be got for love or money. Some Roscommon County Council workers were painting white lines on the road and they had stretched a long line as a guide for where to paint, this line was supported by a number of five-gallon drums! Naturally some people reckoned that, for the sake of accuracy, it would be better if the line was lying on the road, the Council workers are probably still wondering what happened to their drums!

None of this concerned us, as we were in a sailing boat with no engine, however at the end of the week the Rally committee came up trumps and awarded us second place over all, the prize being a Clinton outboard engine.

Newry Canal

In my opinion at present the Association has three major hands-on restoration projects, the Boyne navigation, the Newry Canal and the Ram's Island project, they are all very different but what they share is volunteer enthusiasm. The present chair of Newry Branch is Peter Maxwell who without question leads from the front and by example.

I've stood at a lock on a Saturday morning and viewed the ivy clad walls, the bushes growing fed by the mortar and in some cases trees growing out of the lock walls causing unimaginable damage to the stonework. I've also viewed that lock in mid afternoon astonished at the transformation, vegetation removed, walls cleaned and once again these historic structures revealed in full splendour. Bridges have had the same treatment, even the grass along the roadside trimmed to show off unique arched structures built without mixers, cranes and dumpers, a testament to those navvies of a bygone age. No one is ordered about, coffee and lunch is served, friendships are made and most importantly of all; the work is done.

The Newry navigation is the oldest in all these islands, hence its importance , this was the project where the great engineers of western Europe learnt their trade so any work on these structures requires careful monitoring. The Department of the Environment, built heritage division are the custodians; it is fair to say they were initially nervous of this well meaning bunch of do gooders, now a trust has been built up between both parties and after a mid week telephone call, the project leader acts on the advice received and ensures the job is carried out in accordance with the advice received. Amazing discoveries have been revealed; the deal planking in the bottom of the lock preserved since the canal was refurbished in 1801, some of the lock gate mechanisms that had fallen from the rotten gates now preserved and securely stored waiting refitting for the day this historic waterway will reopen.

The sceptics smile sarcastically at any suggestion of re-opening citing as they see insurmountable problems such as the low bridges in Newry; they obviously haven't seen lifting bridges, swing bridges or what about simply dropping the canal water level as they have done in other parts of these islands. Some years ago, work was done on the section in Newry from Sand's Mill to Carnbane, new lock gates were fitted but for some unknown reason the project was abandoned and those with no regard for this historic waterway deposited their unwanted shopping trolleys, fridges and a plethora of all sorts of items. The Newry Branch volunteers accepted the challenge and now after months of work clearing debris, gravel, mud and skipfulls of rubbish, the Branch are planning a small boat rally, boats again on this section of canal, the sceptics said it would never happen; hurry up lads I'm waiting to launch my little boat and be part of this historic event.

Carnbane lock before and after vegetation clearing projects

Shannon Boat Rally

Dublin and the Grand Canal Rallies

Padraic O Brolchain

In the 60's and 70's the Dublin Branch of the IWAI had a membership of over 600 and was the dominant force in the IWAI. The main issue was first the prevention of the closure of the Grand Canal and later its restoration as a working waterway.

In 1962 an M boat was brought into Dublin from Hazelhatch, the journey from the 12th to the 1st lock took over 12 hours with a support team of about six people. In 1963 there was a small-boat rally on the circle line in Dublin. There had been previous Rallies but this was the beginning of annual Dublin Rally on the Grand Canal. In 1969 Dublin Corporation abandoned the plan to fill in the canal over a sewer and finally decided to tunnel alongside the canal.

At that time CIE was responsible for canal maintenance and the minimum was being done and the next battle was to persuade people to use the canal as it was in a very poor condition. Although the first rallies were small affairs, Dublin branch of the IWAI committed to making the boat rally an annual event with two objectives, the first was to highlight the poor condition of the canal, and the second was to force the opening of the lifting bridge in the Grand Canal basin.

A former Grand Canal barge restored as the Killucan project barge

Opinions within the IWAI were divided on the issue of the lifting bridge. One school believed that we should preserve the right of taller boats to have passage into the inner part of the basin. There was an alternate view that if the bridge was made into a fixed bridge with proper clearance, the inner basin would then be accessible only to canal boats. There was a fear that the rising demand for marina space on the East Coast would mean that sea going boats would swamp the basin before canal based boats got a chance to establish themselves. In 1988 Dublin city staged a Millennium celebration and a major boat rally was planned to mark the occasion. More than 80 boats signed up for the trip. A lot of lessons were learned, particularly in the matter of water management. It took

The Shannon Rally in Athlone

from 7.00 am until after midnight to get the fleet from the 12th lock to Mespil road. In the process Baggot Street was flooded and one of the short stretches near the Barge Inn dried out for more than an hour.

This rally was a huge success in that it raised the level of awareness of the canal among the public and the local authorities. It also established the idea among boat owners, that Dublin was accessible by canal. The rally evolved, with first the inclusion of a trip up the Liffey to Islandbridge, the limit of navigation, and also on at least one occasion a sea trip for some boats across Dublin Bay to Dun Laoghaire. Some adventurous boats made their way into Spencer Dock, the terminus of the Royal Canal. At the time one had to choose the moment with care, entering at low tide to get below the overhead obstructions, and then waiting for the tide to drop again to exit. By the year

2000 it was possible to stage a canals of Dublin Rally without the inclusion of a trip up the Royal. This trip was made not without difficulty and only with a small number of boats, but it was another beginning.

The story will continue, in 1983 we had a dream. Today it is good to see that so much of what we had hoped for has come to be. Boats can travel through Dublin from the Royal to the Grand Canal, Ringsend Basin now has live-aboard boats, the lifting bridge is fixed but with adequate air draft for canal boats. Outreach projects are in place to increase awareness of the amenity value of the canals among local residents.

There is still a lot to do, but without the dedication of those who fought and worked hard to bring their boats up first one and then the other canal into Dublin, we would not have what is there today.

Royal Canal Rally 1999

Padraic O Brolchain

During the time when I was chairman of the Dublin Branch of the IWAI, Eddie Slane, the then chairman of the Dublin Branch of the RCAG invited me to travel on his boat across the new aqueduct over the M50. While travelling through the deep sinking we encountered a washing machine in the canal. Eddie said "we'll have to organise a

Ruth Delany filming the 1999 RCAG rally

work party." I replied "No, let us organise a rally and then the OPW (Office of Public Works) will clear it".

Since the take-over of the canals from CIE by the OPW, Dublin Branch had developed a very good relationship with them, rallies had always been used as a prime tool for drawing attention to the canals and the OPW recognised this and gave us every assistance possible.

From the above conversation, grew a commitment to get boats moving on the Royal Canal. There was already a small hire fleet operated by Derek Whelan, some private boats and some who trailed small boats to the canal. There had been some very successful small-boat rallies on the inland stretches but very little around Dublin.

Our first project was to extend the annual Dublin Grand Canal Rally into the Royal Canal from the

Liffey. This was projected for 1996 and we even had received an undertaking from John McKeown of OPW that in the event of failure of a certain swinging railway bridge, he would hire a crane to remove the obstruction for the duration of the rally. Sadly this was not to be, the courage of the RCAG committee failed them.

Paul Kenny as Chairman of Dublin branch used this idea in a subsequent rally to lift boats past the 9th Lock of the Grand Canal at Clondalkin, when this lock was in peril of collapse.

Following this setback, Allen O'Leary, Noel Spaine and Padraic O Brolchain formed a committee in early 1998 to plan a Royal Canal rally from Dublin to the then end of navigation in Abbeyshrule. We decided that it would start at the aqueduct near Blanchardstown. In addition to the usual complexities of booking eminent citizens to appear, we also needed to produce boats. Allen

Noel Spaine welcomes Sean Fitzimons to the 1999 rally

O'Leary who had many contacts in the boating world came up with the idea of inviting the UK based Wilderness Boat club to bring boats over, these boats are all trailable.

Much to our delight they jumped at the offer and with financial support from Irish Ferries we subsidised their journey to Ireland. With their six boats and four from Derek Whelan's fleet we had the core of a presentable rally. Finally there was an entry of over 20 boats.

The rally was planned so that each branch of the RCAG along the route could contribute and have a day in the limelight. The organising committee was startled at the success of the outcome. Newspaper coverage was beyond our wildest dreams, and the Wilderness Boats who had a special routine using light and sound performed after dark, first in Kilcock Harbour and then at other venues. After the first event crowds flocked to each venue. When the fleet arrived at Mullingar there were over 2000 people to greet us. The success was such, that certain politicians who were unable to be present on the day, asked for a re-enactment the following October.

A sad feature of the event was that Eddie Slane did not live to see it happen. A special memorial to Eddie was unveiled at Mullingar during the Rally.

The significance of the 1999 Royal Canal Rally was that the RCAG were no longer a restoration group fighting in the wilderness against the odds. It also gave the different branches along the route a sense of validation for their years of effort, and a degree of pride in a job well done. It was the beginning of the end of the restoration of the Royal Canal.

I.W.A.I Shannon Boat Rally-Early Years

The Inland Waterways Association of Ireland was founded in January 1954, and soon afterwards in February 1954 the Athlone Branch of the IWAI was founded.

Some of the main aims of the Association were then, and still are:-
1. To promote commercial traffic on our Irish rivers and canals.
2. To ensure that their attractions for boating, cruising, fishing and sailing are more widely known.
3. To oppose any obstruction to their free navigation.

The main lessons learned from these campaigns were the importance of using the navigations regularly and to be seen to be using them. In keeping with their aims, listed above, the Association set about organising cruises and encouraging people to take part to "fly the flag" or "walk the right of way" so to speak, to reinforce their right to passage. The sight of a rally of boats served to attract publicity and illustrated the potential of the river to the Shannon-side towns and villages, and further afield.

The importance of the publicity was also recognised as a useful weapon in the Associations campaign armoury.

Two cruises were organised in 1954, one to Lanesborough and another to Clonmacnoise. In 1955 a number of open boats travelled from Athlone to Knockvicar. Clarendon lock was inoperative and the boats had to be hauled over the weir to continue into Lough Key. The rallyists were asked to leave Lough Key by King-Harman's groundsman – saying that it was private property, but they politely ignored his request. Following pressure from the Athlone Branch, Clarendon Lock at Knockvicar was repaired and re-opened by the summer of 1956.

This cleared the way for a Boat Rally from Athlone to Lough Key, with Col. Harry Rice as Commodore in an open boat, and it was held from the 1st to 8th of August 1956, which also coincided with the Carrick on Shannon Rowing Regatta over the August Bank Holiday weekend.

The rallies were mainly of small numbers in open boats, and the rallies travelling from Athlone to Carrick on Shannon and Lough Key coincided with the Carrick-on-Shannon Rowing Regatta, which often had Athlone crews taking part.

The Bridge at Carrick-on-Shannon

In 1961 Athlone Branch IWAI together with the Carrick-on-Shannon Branch IWAI and the Boyle Development Association came together to organise the first of the big Shannon Boat Rallies as we know them today.

"Never before was such riverside activity witnessed at Athlone when pleasure craft of all sizes and types assembled below the Town Bridge, preparatory to the great rally up-river to Lough Key." The official list shows that seventy-one boats took part but, similar to the number of people claiming to have been in the GPO in the Easter Rising, everybody you speak to apparently was on the first rally which would suggest that at least one hundred and fifty boats took part, and it was the greatest mustering of craft ever seen on an Irish inland waterway.

Athlone from the air, showing the docks on the left and the Strand on the right

Esso Petroleum Company supplied the fuel free of charge for all participating craft, which was a major incentive for anyone to enter.

The boats departed from Athlone at 6am on Saturday morning of the 5th August 1961 under the command of Commodore Paddy Flynn in his boat "Barracuda". Syd Shine in "Fox" led the flotilla and they travelled to Jamestown where, above Jamestown Cut, they tried to assemble in line astern for the remaining four miles into Carrick-on-Shannon, but this actually turned out to be a "mad dash with the fast boats haring it to Carrick, swamping the small boats with their wake".

Members of the Carrick-on-Shannon IWAI branch were on the quayside to welcome the participants, and direct them to their moorings. This also appeared not to work too well and was the source of much complaint at the post-mortem meeting.

The Rally moved on to Lough Key on Sunday 6th August where they were entertained at Rockingham by the Boyle Development Association.

Monday being the August Bank Holiday the rally returned to Carrick-on-Shannon for the Carrick Regatta, and a dinner dance which was held on the CIE Cruiser "St Ciaran". The Rowing Regatta also had a Marquee Dance adjacent to the quay.

Tuesday was a free day, and on Wednesday the rally moved down river with stops at Rooskey and Lanesborough, and back to Lough Ree on Friday and Saturday with competitions en route. The presentation of prizes was held at Hodson Bay on Sunday evening August 13th. The winner of the Premier Award on the First Rally in 1961 was R.A. Wright from Newtownards, Co. Down; Boat No. 46; "Kami no Michi".

The 1961 rally was a great success and it gained much publicity from the press, from Pathe News films, and boating magazines. Most of the feedback from entrants to the post-mortem meeting after the Rally was positive, and it focused mainly around the choice of date for the 1962 Rally. Some people wanted to move the date forward into early July either to avoid competition in the media from the RDS Horse Show, or to take part in the Show, while others opted for late July/early August to coincide with business, school, and builder holidays. There were also calls for more activity during the Rally, and for a fairer marking system for the judging of the competitions.

Esso Petroleum Company Ltd came up trumps again and supplied all the fuel free of charge for the 1962 Rally. "Officially" eighty-one boats entered the Rally, but other sources put that number at approximately 110.

Syd Shine, musician and waterways pioneer

Paddy Flynn in "Barracuda" was the Commodore again and Syd Shine in "Fox" led the fleet out of Athlone at 6am on Saturday 28th July 1962 en route to Carrick-on-Shannon. Participants were advised that ample time was allocated for all the fleet to arrive safely in Carrick, and they were asked to desist from the "rat run" and to observe the line astern request for the Jamestown to the Carrick section.

The itinerary followed much the same route and level of activity as in the 1961 rally, and finished with the presentation of prizes at Hodson Bay on Sunday 5th August. H.J.M. Barnes from Cheshire, England, in Boat No. 51, "Senrab II" won the Premier Award in 1962. Things appeared to work better in 1962, with the result that there was very little correspondence to the post-mortem meeting.

1963, and Esso sponsored the fuel again. Paddy Flynn in "Barracuda" was Commodore, and Syd Shine in "Fox" led the flotilla out of Athlone en route to Carrick-on-Shannon at 6am on Saturday 27th July. The fleet were divided into three groups. Each group had a lead boat, which departed on a flag signal at fifteen minute intervals from the Commodores flagship which was anchored in mid stream south of the railway bridge in Athlone.

The itinerary over Sunday and Monday in Lough Key included a Speed Boat race and a Yacht race, Inspection of Boats competition, Man Overboard competition, Treasure Hunt, Barbecue, a Signalling Competition for the Wright Cup, and a Marquee Dance. They held a mooring of small craft competition and an Informal Dinner at Carrick-on-Shannon on Tuesday. The trip to Rooskey included a short detour to Carnadoe and later they held a small craft handling lecture, Semaphore Signalling, and a fishing competition weigh in with a barbecue at Rooskey. The trip to Lanesboro had a fishing competition en route and a local party on arrival.

Over Friday & Saturday there was a Navigation Competition, a Mooring to a Buoy Competition, a Rescue of Dinghy Competition, a Dance and Informal Dinner, and Presentation of Prizes at Hodson Bay on Sunday 4th August. Syd Shine from Athlone in M.B. Fox won the Premier Award for 1963.

1964 started out as a bad year for the Inland Waterways Association of Ireland with the death of two of its most prominent founder members

Rosemary Furlong participating in an early rally

Esso were still sponsoring the fuel, and the rally travelled north to Lough Key with stopovers in Carrick-on-Shannon, Rooskey, Tarmonbarry, Lanesborough, Athlone, and further southwards to Clonmacnoise, which was a new venue.

Dermot O'Cleary in M.Y. "Fresia" was Commodore; Norman Furlong and Bill Child were the two Vice Commodores. The "Official" Entry List shows that one hundred and sixty boats took part, – a record.

Lieut. Cdr. J.J. St. John Earle in Boat No. 45, "Blue Waterman" won the Premier Award in 1964.

The Esso Sponsorship was a major factor in the success of the early rallies. Without the support of Esso the organisers would have had a much more difficult job in attracting the large numbers of boats to enter and come back each year.

The extent and value of the fuel sponsorship can be calculated from the quantity of fuel provided to the 1964 rally :-

– Vincent Delany in January and Harry Rice in May. Life goes on and the Shannon Boat Rally Committee was showing all the signs of a modern progressive organisation, learning from the previous rallies. They produced a folded, glossy, coloured brochure with all the general information for entrants on the front and a promotional narrative on the River Shannon interwoven with a bit of history on the back. Bord Failte would have been proud of it.

Overall the organisation of the Rally appeared to be tighter and better controlled. The literature for the entrants and the movement of the fleet appeared to have benefited from their previous experience.

	Petrol	Mixture	Diesel	T.V.O.
Dublin	560	160	190	80
Athlone (Outwards)	822	875	928	355
Carrick on Shannon Outwards)	410	193	225	132
Carrick on Shannon (Homewards)	563	866	153	225
Athlone (Homewards)	993	975	645	380
Total (9730 Gallons)	3348	3069	2141	1172

It's difficult to expect that any company could sustain that level of sponsorship indefinitely, but our thanks must go to Paddy Dolan and Dermot Jordan of Esso for securing that level of sponsorship for the Rally for five years.

Refuelling at Carrick from the Esso tanker

Esso discontinued their fuel sponsorship in 1966 / 67 amid great fears that the Rally numbers would then collapse, but the Rally was sufficiently well founded by then and while the numbers fell back to around eighty boats they remained at that level for many more years, fluctuating between seventy and a hundred up to the present day. For the first six rallies the Commodore had always been selected from Athlone Branch IWAI. In 1967 Billy Whyte from Carrick-on-Shannon Branch IWAI was selected as Commodore and this was the start of the system of alternating the selection of Commodore between the two Branches.

Other changes started to take place over the next few years – the long voyage from Athlone to Carrick-on-Shannon on the same day was abolished, instead, the location for the Rally also alternated each year from the "Athlone end" to the "Carrick end" which also served to abolish the 6.00am starts. Slowly over the years the Rally has become more leisurely and family orientated.

Rosemary Furlong presenting the Harry Rice Cup

Our thanks must go to the committees and participants of those early years who set up the Rally on such a firm foundation. The list of committee members, helpers at locks and harbours, judges, and general gofers is endless and listing their names is fraught with the danger of omission, and we thank them all collectively. However the names that appear in the records year after year as the driving forces in the early Rallies whom we also thank for their vision and perseverance are:-

Athlone Branch: – Paddy Flynn, Syd Shine, Harry & Cynthia Rice, Norman & Rosemary Furlong, Mick Mannion, Dolly Behan, Mai Cauldwell, Dermot O'Cleary, Michael Webb, and apologies to those I failed to mention.

Carrick-on-Shannon Branch: – Tom Maher, Bill Child, Doc Farrell, Billy Whyte, Angus Dunne,

John Conway, and apologies also to those I failed to mention.

Boyle Development Association: – Tom Carroll, Jimmy Flaherty.

We also owe thanks to all the Rally Committees and participants in the intervening years from 1961 to 2010, those who sustained, modified and strengthened the Rally organisation and status, which allows us now to celebrate 50 years of the Shannon Boat Rally.

"Blackthorn" moored in Shannon Harbour

Shannon Harbour Rally

Padraic O Brochain

The annual Shannon Harbour Canal Boat Rally takes place on the nearest weekend to the Summer Solstice – the 21st June. The first rally was held in 1971.

Capt. Kelly Rogers, Duncan Bain, Gay and Kathleen Bush and later Noel Murphy were deeply involved in the early years. They formed a rally committee which included local residents, most importantly Mrs. Guinan of Guinan's bar and her son Peter. Other stalwarts at that time were the Thomas's, Queenie and Jim, who kept a caravan but no boat and Jeff and Mona White whose boat "The Willows" rarely strayed far from the harbour, and Sean Bailey with his canal boat "Dabu" (2B).

The Canal Boat Rally was exactly that – a gathering of canal boats (one did not use the word barge). The harbour was cleared (not a difficult task in those days) and berths were allocated in advance to each and every 60 ft traditional canal boat that entered. Sean Fitzsimons with "Ye Iron Lung", Sid Shine's "Fox", Donnchadh Kennedy's "Sequoia" and "Palo Alto", George Speirs' 95B and others. These were all converted canal boats and the proud owners were expected to have open house for all visitors on the Sunday of the rally. This was a very popular event with people who lived in the area, as there were still many people around who remembered the old boats in their heyday. It was after all, only ten years since traffic had finally ceased.

On Friday night the fleet gathered, the committee had a final meeting and possibly imbibed, and on Saturday morning the event commenced. Water-sports for children of all ages, included water polo with dinghies and broom handles, rowing races and other water based novelty events. These were held in the harbour and the decks of the canal boats (barges!!!) provided a viewing platform. Boats were inspected and awarded points mainly related to safety and engine and bilge cleanliness. Most of the wives thought the galley was the main focus – it wasn't. On Sunday there was a religious service usually in the open air, followed by land sports on the green in front of the old hotel and harbour-master's house.

Meanwhile in the background there was a fun-fair, a visiting chipper and in 1972 very memorably, helicopter rides sponsored by Odlums. Importantly of course there were the two pubs, Guinans and Gleesons.

The Rally was run by a committee made up largely of Dublin based people. While it was under the IWAI banner, it was independent and had its own funding, such as it was. The committee had only one function, the running of the rally. In 1985 a separate Shannon Harbour Branch of the IWAI was formed and they and the rally committee finally merged.

Before all this happened, in the early 1980's management of the rally descended on Eoghan Ganly and Brian Hatfield, both owners of new steel boats built in Lowtown by Paul Doran. Cyril Irwin was

Harbour Master's House at Shannon Harbour

elected honorary Commodore, a post he held for many years. His boat Cyan, named after his daughter, was an excellent venue for the committee party. The original committee had mostly retired from the scene after more than ten years hard work. By this time Shannon Harbour's boat population had increased and it was becoming difficult to accommodate the boats for the rally, the big canal boats had to moor on the periphery. Space for water-sports was restricted.

Brian and Eoghan felt that by virtue of the fact that they were not bargees, they did not have the proper status to ask people to clear the harbour for the rally. Padraic and Sue O Brolchain (The "Bishop Whelan" 66M) and Michael and Laura Hodgins (34M) joined the committee and their first contribution was to initiate a pre-rally clearance of the harbour, with the temporary relocation of boats whose owners did not intend being at the rally. There was a significant number who

Picture of barge struggling to get through a lock on the Grand Canal

were politely asked to move or be moved. This was not a totally easy process, but ownership of a 60 ft long steel and concrete monster weighing over 50 tons did confer a certain degree of the necessary "clout" in delicate negotiations.

Later when Padraic became Rally Chairman, his first resolve was to put the committee on a firm financial footing. Hitherto the committee members had frequently to put their hands in their pockets for prizes, props and so on. A barn dance was organised in Dublin, and the proceeds established the necessary float to fund future rallies. Everyone enjoyed the night so much that for some years afterwards an annual event was held in Dublin, we were no longer desperate for funds, and it was good fun.

The committee grew, Jack and Aideen Roberts ("Sequoia" 40M), Denis and Nuala Treacy, Pat

and Anna Henry, Les Saunders (41M) swelled the ranks and each and every one had a contribution to make. This group ran the rally for a number of years. The pattern varied only slightly, a fancy dress night was added to the programme, and there were various different events from time to time.

Paul Doran and Jeanne Hollinshead who had worked at building and repairing boats in Lowtown Marina, moved their operation to Belmont and bought an 80 foot barge, "Liverpool" as a live-aboard. She became a fixture on the quay, and the centre for rally activities for many years. On the Sunday Liverpool was taken over by the Ladies who allocated the vast collection of prizes and trophies which were presented during the afternoon.

During this period, ownership of the canal was transferred from CIE, the IWAI became incorporated and Shannon Harbour Branch, initially under John Johnson as Chairman became a viable group. Many of the rally committee also joined the branch in 1985 and eventually it was decided to hand over the running of the rally to the Shannon Harbour Branch of the IWAI.

The harbour became more crowded and the character of the rally changed. Paul Kenny was joined by a group representing the next generation, Ann Hollinshead, Eoin O Brolchain, Dave Smith and friends. They moved on and were followed by Greg Whelan, Brenda Ainsworth, and others. Pat and Anna Henry who had been involved for

Overhead gantries in the shed at Shannon Harbour

were able to get good moorings in the harbour for the duration of the Rally. There are new faces, including Damien Buckley a canal boat owner from Tullamore. The recent work by Waterways Ireland and the introduction of a 5 day rule has ensured that the harbour is not clogged by unoccupied boats, and the new amenity block is a considerable addition.

*Smartie racing, for the uninitiated, involves embedding the confectionery of that name in a heap of flour and contestants have to retrieve a sweet without using their hands. "A messy business with lots of floury faces."

many years took over aided by their son Victor and friend Donna. It was at that time that Frank and Nuala O'Gorman introduced a barbecue as the main event on Saturday night, fancy dress optional. This has become the main event at the Rally. Water Sports became very difficult, because the harbour was so crowded. Land sports became less varied as health and safety issues started to dominate. First, barrel rolling, then water bucket races and pillow fights died and now running races, egg and spoon and smartie* races are the main events.

The rally continues to be an important event on the IWAI calendar and the 2013 rally attracted over 70 entries, about half of whom came especially for the week-end. This year the event was enhanced by the arrival of a number of Heritage Boats (old canal boats and others) most of whom

Lough Derg Rally;

(Compiled from an article by Natalie Magowan)

The first minuted meeting of Lough Derg Branch in February 1971 "considered the Shannon Rally had outlived its attraction" (wonder what the present Shannon Boat Rally Officers would have to say about that!) and further stated that it was time Lough Derg became better known to boat hirers. Among the possible sponsors suggested were Esso and Carroll's cigarettes. It was decided the first effort should not be too ambitious and could take the form of a conducted tour around the lake over a weekend. A rally sub-committee was formed under the chairmanship of Mr W O'Leary and was held over the weekend of 26 and 27th June 1971. Boats assembled in Kilgarvan on

Killaloe, Lough Derg

the Friday evening and proceeded to Scarriff on the Saturday and dispersed on the Sunday.

At this time the pier at Kilgarvan was under construction though it was hoped to moor fifteen boats, help was offered and provided by Kilgarvan Angling Club; to all intent everything must have gone well and a sum of £13 was raised and presented to the anglers to purchase a new trophy. I understand that cordial relationship still exists as the April Kilgarvan barbecue still exists!

The following year the Branch was obviously growing in confidence and the decision was taken to extend the event to three nights. Kilgarvan and Scarriff were again visited; indeed Kilgarvan gets a special mention for its 'wonderful reception' such was the success this time around that a second rally was organised for September. The following year saw organised activities being intro-

duced, an inspection of boats and gear, by 1973 there were suggestions being made that the rally should be a seven day event, though I understand that event didn't materialise. The Branch issued an invitation to the Shannon Rally to visit Lough Derg in two years time, 1975. A mini rally was planned to Ballinderry over the Whit weekend in 1974 but according to the minutes some enjoyed the hospitality to excess as the following minutes suggest; "a disturbance took place during the stay in Kilgarvan"!

Over the following years the rally subcommittee organised various events, rallies, barbecues; all obviously successful. The 1975 rally certainly seems to have been a huge success as it attracted some eighty-four boats, thirty-five from Derg Branch while forty-nine were from other branches. Competitions now played a major part of the organisation and numerous trophies were competed for, if I told you there were fourteen committee meetings organised to arrange the rally, well it had to be successful! Ladies and Junior Committees were established, I like the duty assigned to the juniors; cutting the cheese for the wine and cheese reception, good job they didn't allow them to sample the wine or a young committee member, Miss Natalie Duffy might have been tipsy! The rally had truly arrived; the tremendous successful organisation we experience today was established, firstly in the 1980's it was a week in August while in 2002 it became established in July. I finish with a quote from Natalie; "The rally has evolved over the years but its basic premise remains the same, an enjoy-

Larkins, often home to the Lough Derg branch

able week cruising Lough Derg in the company of fellow boaters. It is hard to describe to others the fun and companionship on a rally and how if they never go on another holiday your kids will beg to come back year after year, I know I have been that kid and I'm still doing the rally!"

Devenish Island on Lower Lough Erne

Lough Erne Rally

Colin Beattie

The Lough Erne Rally was started in 1963 by a committee made up from the Upper Lough Erne area and Belturbet, at that time no IWAI Branches existed in either area. The Committee included from Upper Lough Erne; Lord Erne, Wesley Dawson and Hubert Brown and from Belturbet – Victor Barham, James Brady and possibly Fred Smith.

There were a couple of Cruises in company before 1965 when the Erne Rally officially commenced. In 1965 Pat McGuinness and I were seconded on to the Erne Rally Committee and I think by that

time Ian Eadie from Upper Lough Erne area had joined and also a man called Edwin Woodhouse (his son is now a great supporter). By that time there were approximately ten to twelve boats participating in the event. As the years went by, more boats arrived and the Erne Rally became the group which opened up the Lake – the Councils of Cavan and Enniskillen providing facilities as the Rally cruised further down the Lake eventually reaching Belleek, indeed this was how the lake became more and more developed in those early days.

Each year the Erne Rally grew in size and cruised new waters and then hire boats started to arrive on the lake; entrants hired boats and joined the rally. At this stage people like Noreen Cooper, Harry West, Jack Leahy and Mervyn Dennison started to take an interest and the success spread further south and north and the rally had entrants numbering up to over fifty participants with some years seventy! The committee always tried to change the route each year and included as many sports and other activities as could be squeezed into four days. Robert Maitland was an enthusiastic organiser of sports and Pat McGuinness with Albert Broomhead organized tug-o-war featured for many years even across the Arney River! Safety was always paramount and I remember there was a tragedy at the Arney River when a young vet lost his life though not a participant in the rally.

On the 25th anniversary Pat McGuinness was elected Chairman and I was elected Commodore, we published a book with articles from people from North and South. After the Ballinamore Ballyconnell canal was restored one rally went as far as Carrick-on-Shannon joining up with the local branch of IWAI from that area.

2015 will be the fiftieth rally and as far as I can establish I have taken part in all of them. Gerry Mackeral, a stalwart rally supporter and myself have been invited to be joint Commodores for that very special event.

Past and Present Officers of the Association

Compiled by Ruth Delany

Year of Election	President	Vice-President	Hon. Secretary	Hon. Treasurer
1954	Harry Rice		Vincent Delany & L.M.Goodbody	G.C.M. Thompson
1955	Harry Rice		Peter Denham	G.C.M. Thompson
1956	Harry Rice		Peter Denham	G.C.M. Thompson
1957	Harry Rice		Peter Denham	Douglas Mellon
1958	Harry Rice		Peter Denham	Douglas Mellon
1959	Jack Henry		Peter Denham	Douglas Mellon
1960	Jack Henry		Peter Denham	Douglas Mellon
1961	Jack Henry		Peter Denham	Fred Waterstone
1962	Dermot O'Cleary		Peter Denham	Fred Waterstone
1963	Dermot O'Cleary		Peter Denham	Fred Waterstone
1964	Dermot O'Cleary		Peter Denham	Fred Waterstone
1965	Dermot O'Cleary		Peter Denham	Fred Waterstone
1966	Dermot O'Cleary		Peter Denham	Fred Waterstone
1967	Alf Delany		Sean Glennon	Fred Waterstone
1968	Alf Delany		Sean Glennon	Fred Waterstone
1969	Alf Delany		Sean Glennon	Fred Waterstone
1970	Alf Delany		Sean Glennon	Fred Waterstone
1971	Alf Delany		Jeremy Addis	Maureen Browne
1972	Alf Delany		Jeremy Addis	Maureen Browne

Year of Election	President	Vice-President	Hon. Secretary	Hon. Treasurer
1973	Alf Delany		Jeremy Addis	Maureen Browne
1974	Alf Delany		Jeremy Addis	Maureen Browne
1975	Alf Delany		Jeremy Addis	Maureen Browne
1976	Alf Delany		Pat Benson	Terence Mallagh
1977	Alf Delany		Duncan Bain	Terence Mallagh
1978	Bill Child		Duncan Bain	Cyril Irwin
1979	Bill Child		Alan Algeo	Cyril Irwin
1980	Bill Child		Alan Algeo	Cyril Irwin
1981	Ruth Heard	John Suitor	Alan Algeo	Cyril Irwin
1982	Ruth Heard	John Suitor	Alan Algeo	Maureen Browne
1983	Ruth Heard	John Suitor	Michael Webb	Maureen Browne
1984	John Suitor	Peter Hanna	Michael Webb	Maureen Browne
1985	John Suitor	Peter Hanna	Michael Webb	Joyce Waterhouse
1986	John Suitor	Peter Hanna	Liam D'Arcy	Joyce Waterhouse
1987	Peter Hanna	Damien Delaney	Liam D'Arcy	Joyce Waterhouse
1988	Peter Hanna	Damien Delaney	Liam D'Arcy	Alan Waterhouse
1989	Peter Hanna	Damien Delaney	Peadar Canavan	Alan Waterhouse
1990	Damien Delaney	Des Leyden	Peadar Canavan	Alan Waterhouse
1991	Damien Delaney	Des Leyden	Peadar Canavan	Mary Gallagher
1992	Damien Delaney	Des Leyden	Dermot Murphy	Mary Gallagher
1993	Des Leyden	Ian Bath	Dermot Murphy	Reggie Redmond
1994	Des Leyden	Liam D'Arcy	Colin Becker	Reggie Redmond
1995	Des Leyden	Liam D'Arcy	Colin Becker	Reggie Redmond
1996	Liam D'Arcy	Colin Becker	Catherine Malone	Reggie Redmond
1997	Liam D'Arcy	Colin Becker	Catherine Malone	Reggie Redmond
1998	Liam D'Arcy	Colin Becker	Catherine Malone	Reggie Redmond

Year of Election	President	Vice-President	Hon. Secretary	Hon. Treasurer
1999	Colin Becker	Donal O'Siocháin	Rosaleen Miller	Reggie Redmond
2000	Colin Becker	Donal O'Siocháin	Rosaleen Miller	Reggie Redmond
2001	Colin Becker	Donal O'Siocháin	Rosaleen Miller	Reggie Redmond
2002	Donal O'Siocháin	Brian Cassells	Ruth Corrigan	Reggie Redmond
2003	Donal O'Siochain	Brian Cassells	Maurice Kerr	Reggie Redmond
2004	Donal O'Siocháin	Brian Cassells	Carmel Meegan	John Corrigan
2005	Brian Cassells	Paul Garland	Carmel Meegan	John Corrigan
2006	Brian Cassells	Paul Garland	Carmel Meegan	John Corrigan
2007	Brian Cassells	Paul Garland	Carmel Meegan	John Corrigan
2008	Paul Garland	Gregory Whelan	Carmel Meegan	John Corrigan
2009	Paul Garland	Gregory Whelan	Carmel Meegan	John Corrigan
2010	Paul Garland	Gregory Whelan	Derry Smyth	John Corrigan
2011	Gregory Whelan	Carmel Meegan	Derry Smyth	John Corrigan
2012	Gregory Whelan	Carmel Meegan	Derry Smyth	Paddy Bowen
2013	Carmel Meegan	Derry Smith	Kay Baxter	Jean Kennedy
2014	Carmel Meegan	John Dolan	Kay Baxter	Jean Kennedy

The IWAI at work

Elsewhere I have listed some of our major ongoing projects but that is by no means the complete picture. Virtually every branch has a project, Corrib surveying the lake, Lagan revealing the unique flight of four locks at Sprucefield, Kildare with their M boat refurbishment, Derg with their work parties even installing jetties and an ambitious project known as CSIG, Charts Special Interest Group whose aim is to produce a paper and electronic chart which will depict obstacles and list valuable information to enhance any waterway journey.

There are a plethora of events taking place throughout the year, walks and talks in winter, all the year round litter lifts, boat rallies, the list is endless, indeed a quick look at the events programme reveals the diversity of branch activities. Our heritage is our priority; some are amassing photographs, written records, recorded conversations of long retired boatmen, amateur films portraying the dying commercial life and the leisure activities of yesteryear. Members painstakingly restore boats, a labour of love yet vital to record designs often conceived in minds and never recorded on paper. Coracles, skiffs, cots and currachs are be-

ing constructed in the Boyne Valley, in Gilford Co Down and places I just don't know about, oh I nearly forgot, one of our latest additions is a bee garden, where do you ask; on the Newry Canal of course!

Up and down the country, meetings are being convened; records kept by teams of volunteers, many are virtually unknown people who have a passion for our Association, a love to share knowledge with like minded people and a passion for our waterways. I often hear the remark, what can IWAI do for me, other than the magazine, the web site and a few other incentives what do I get for my money? What a selfish way to view a body that has worked tirelessly for 60 years fighting to keep the waterways open for all to enjoy; it should never be what am I getting, rather what can I contribute for the good of my fellow boater!

The Association needs more members, people who will contribute, when we lobby those in authority they often ask how many members do you represent, this is where numbers count, everyone can do something, what new activities have I omitted to list?

Brian Cassells

achievements ... progress ... attainments ... deeds ... accomplishments ... successes

179

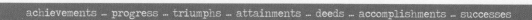

Inland Waterways Association Of Ireland

Founded in 1954

Voluntary association with 22 branches nationwide

Represents interests of waterway users and enthusiasts

Organises boat rallies, social events, training courses and educational activities

Promotes conservation, restoration, development and use of the waterways

Liases with roi & ni governments, navigation authorities, local authorities & state agencies on waterway issues

Produces quarterly magazine; inland waterways news

On line shop

Join on line today @ www.iwai.ie

Telephone Numbers; Roi Low Call; 1890 924 001

Uk Tel; 028 3832 5329

International 00 353 (0) 91 589 333